# WILLA CATHER

Women Writers

General Editors: *Eva Figes* and *Adele King*

**Published titles:**

*Margaret Atwood*, Barbara Hill Rigney
*Anne Brontë*, Elizabeth Langland
*Charlotte Brontë*, Pauline Nestor
*Emily Brontë*, Lyn Pykett
*Fanny Burney*, Judy Simons
*Willa Cather*, Susie Thomas
*Sylvia Plath*, Susan Bassnett
*Christina Stead*, Diana Brydon
*Eudora Welty*, Louise Westling
*Women in Romanticism*, Meena Alexander

**Forthcoming:**

*Jane Austen*, Meenakshi Mukherjee
*Elizabeth Barrett Browning*, Marjorie Stone
*Elizabeth Bowen*, Phyllis Lassner
*Ivy Compton Burnett*, Kathy Gentile
*Colette*, Diana Holmes
*Emily Dickinson*, Joan Kirkby
*George Eliot*, Kristin Brady
*Mrs Gaskell*, Jane Spencer
*Doris Lessing*, Barbara Hill Rigney
*Katherine Mansfield*, Diane DeBell
*Christina Rossetti*, Linda Marshall
*Jean Rhys*, Carol Rumens
*Stevie Smith*, Catherine Civello
*Muriel Spark*, Judith Sproxton
*Edith Wharton*, Katherine Joslin
*Virginia Woolf*, Clare Hanson

Women Writers

# Willa Cather

## Susie Thomas

BARNES & NOBLE BOOKS
Savage, Maryland

First published in the USA 1990 by
  BARNES & NOBLE BOOKS
  8705 Bollman Place
  Savage, Maryland 20763

  ISBN 0–389–20882–5
  ISBN 0–389–20883–3 (Pbk)

Printed in the People's Republic of China

Library of Congress Cataloging in Publication Data

Thomas, Susie
  Willa Cather/Susie Thomas.
      p.     cm. — (Women writers)
  Bibliography: p.
  Includes index.
  ISBN 0–389–20882–5                          ISBN 0–389–20883–3 (pbk)

  1. Cather, Willa, 1873–1947 — Criticism and interpretation.
I. Title. II. Series.
PS3505.A87Z87 1990
813′.52—dc20                                          89–34033
                                                     CIP


USA EDITION

#19742580

# Contents

# Acknowledgements

I would very much like to thank Professor Alan G. Hill of Royal Holloway and Bedford New College, London University and Dr M. Cotsell of Delaware University, for their criticism and continued encouragement. I would also like to thank Stewart Spencer for his helpful comments on Willa Cather and Wagner.

Due to stipulations in Cather's will, which prohibit the publication of her letters, it is difficult to gain access to her correspondence. I would like to acknowledge a grant from London University's Central Research Fund which enabled me to visit America for this purpose. Of the many libraries which responded to my enquiries about Cather material I am particularly grateful to: Amherst College Library; Bailey/Howe Library, University of Vermont; Clifton Waller Barret Library, University of Virginia; Beinecke Library, Yale University; Bentley Historical Library, University of Michigan; Boatwright Memorial Library, University of Richmond; Butler Library, Columbia University; Houghton Library, Harvard University; Huntington Library; Nebraska State Historical Society; Newberry Library; New York Public Library; William R. Perkins Library, Duke University; Phillips Exeter Academy; Pierpont Morgan Library; Princeton University Library; Sterling Memorial Library, Yale University; Willa Cather Pioneer Memorial Museum and Educational Foundation.

The author and publishers wish to thank the following who have kindly given permission for the use of copyright material: Virago Press Ltd, with Houghton Mifflin Company for extracts from *Song of the Lark*

# Editors' Preface

The study of women's writing has been long neglected by a male critical establishment both in academic circles and beyond. As a result, many women writers have either been unfairly neglected, or have been marginalised in some way, so that their true influence and importance has been ignored. Other women writers have been accepted by male critics and academics, but on terms which seem, to many women readers of this generation, to be false or simplistic. In the past the internal conflicts involved in being a woman in a male-dominated society have been largely ignored by readers of both sexes, and this has affected our reading of women's work. The time has come for a serious re-assessment of women's writing in the light of what we understand today.

This series is designed to help in that re-assessment. All the books are written by women, because we believe that men's understanding of feminist critique is only, at best, partial. And besides, men have held the floor quite long enough.

Eva Figes
Adele King

For my mother and in memory of my father.

# Introduction

When Cather was asked to comment on Nebraska as a 'storehouse of literary material' her answer, as the interviewer remarked, was 'less than conciliatory': "'If a true artist was born in a pig pen and raised in a sty, he would still find plenty of inspiration for his work.'"[1] Cather happened to grow up in the Midwest and she wrote most convincingly about the things she knew well. Later, she wrote about other places too but critics have concentrated almost exclusively on her portrayal of the frontier. Being classified as a regional novelist has seriously damaged Cather's reputation and prevented her work from receiving the recognition it deserves.[2]

This limiting categorisation is the result of the preoccupation, on both sides of the Atlantic, with what it means to be American. Cather has been one of the casualties in what the poet, Randall Jarrell, described as 'the long, dreary imaginary war in which America and the Present are fighting against Europe and the Past.'[3] As she was not engaged in the crusade to go one 'hundred per cent American',[4] her work has been seen as tangential or irrelevant to the main current of American fiction. It was particularly amongst her male compatriots that the call for an authentic American literature was the most vociferous and, perhaps as a consequence, the dominant tradition in America has been not simply male but aggressively masculine. It is not surprising, then, that Cather – a woman, and a writer concerned with the European heritage – should have been pushed aside.

Virginia Woolf, in her essay on American Fiction in 1925, commented on the uneasy relation of American writers to

the English literary tradition and made a revealing parallel:
'One is reminded constantly of the attitude of another race,
till lately subject and still galled by the memory of its
chains. Women writers have to meet many of the same
problems that beset Americans.'[5] But what of the American
woman writer? Sherwood Anderson's attempt to shape a
distinctive, indigenous art by repeating hypnotically, 'I am
the American man', was evidently unavailable to her. Cather
at first found the consciousness of race and sex an almost
insuperable barrier; the writers she admired were not only
male, they were not American; women, she felt, were only
capable of writing about love and marriage and, in any case,
what could possibly be said about Nebraska?

Her mature achievement rests on her ability to transcend
the limitations of gender and nationality; her capacity to
make the local universal and to speak of men and women.
She developed a unique voice; neither insistently American nor specifically female. Ironically, her unpromising
Midwestern origins gave her a way forward; the lives
of her immigrant neighbours provided her with a link
between the Old World and the New and this continuity of
culture became one of her central themes. She also refused
to be limited to traditionally female subjects; although she
created some of the most compelling female characters in
twentieth-century literature, she employed male narrators
and protaganists when it suited her purpose; she ventured into the previously male preserve of war and the
almost exclusively male territory of the West.

Unlike so many of her compatriots, who rejected European forms in their drive to forge an authentic American
literature, Cather was interested in the combination of
European forms and American experience. Until recently,
only the latter has received much attention. This study
attempts to show the particular contribution Cather made
as a woman writing about the American scene; to analyse
her profound and enriching response to European literature,

music and painting; and to show how her particular cultural awareness influenced her experiments with narrative form and the development of her distinctive style. The pervasive tendency to marginalise women's writing, by applying limiting classifications, is nowhere more apparent than in Cather's relegation to the rank of old-fashioned local colourist. I intend to show how her work acts as a corrective to the aggressively masculine tendencies in American literature and, by placing her work in its proper cultural context, I hope that she will emerge, clearly, as a major writer of universal significance.

# 1 Willa Cather 1873–1947

> Alack,
> That I have worn so many winters out,
> And know not now what name to call myself!
> Quoted by Cather in a letter to Louise Pound in 1897[1]

For some reason Cather lied about her age. She was adamant, even with old friends who knew it wasn't true, that she was born in 1876. It is a harmless, almost pathetically small lie, and yet a curious one for someone who was not apparently in the least vain. Nor was her name Willa. She was christened Wilella, but understandably disliked it. In adolescence she called herself William and in her sixties she still sometimes signed letters, Willie. The public image of Cather as a straightforward, self-assured woman – all rosy cheeks and sturdy walking shoes – is even more misleading than public images usually are.

Despite five biographies and the memoirs of several contemporaries, her life remains an enigma.[2] The initial difficulty results from Cather's extreme reticence about her personal life and has been compounded by the willingness of her friends to enter into this conspiracy of silence. She held the awkward, albeit justified, view that the artist and the woman are discrete entities and that her private life was her exclusive concern. In sharp contrast to many modern, and in particular male, American authors she adhered to Flaubert's dictum: 'L'homme n'est rien, l'oeuvre est tout.' She gave few interviews (and those are mostly early); shunned all forms of public appearance, and did her best to make sure that this rigorous integrity was maintained after her death by destroying her manuscripts, all personal letters in her control and prohibiting the publication of those which remained. Her friends, in deference to her wishes, largely confined themselves to discussions of her career. Edith Lewis, for example, a companion for nearly forty years, maintains a resolutely impersonal tone throughout her memoir and guarded Cather's posthumous reputation like a dragon breathing fire over buried treasure.

Secrecy is bound to provoke speculation, often of an unwholesome kind. Cather's childhood, though, was unexceptional. She herself said that her memories of that time were the safest ones she had.[3] She was the eldest of seven children in a middle-class, Virginian family that was permanently short of money. Her father, Charles Cather, was a gentle, humorous and handsome man; her mother, Mary Virginia (neé Boak), an imperious and energetic Southern belle who disciplined her children with a rawhide whip but also allowed them considerable freedom. Although Cather and her mother sometimes clashed they remained close.[4]

When she was nine the family went West. They left the fluted columns of Willow Shade in the Shenandoah Valley in order to join Charles Cather's father and brother who had already moved to Nebraska. The sudden transplantation from an established and conventional society to raw prairie was a traumatic event and Cather, at first, found herself alone and weeping amid the alien corn. In 1884 they left the ranch in Webster County and settled into the white frame house in Red Cloud where Cather spent the rest of her childhood and often returned to visit her parents.

The bustling little town of Red Cloud (only three years older than Cather) and the surrounding country, appear frequently in her work. Nebraskan friends and neighbours too provided her with prototypes for many of her characters.[5] James Shively refers to the 'curious picture of the Willa Cather of that time': 'a sort of wild girl of the west, riding across the prairies and listening openmouthed to the tales of the immigrant settlers.'[6] But this is not, as Shively suggests, just a bookseller's blurb; she certainly was attracted to the European pioneers and, because of her own experience of being uprooted, she identified strongly with their sense of exile. Through the French, German and Bohemian families, she first became attached to Europe and its art. She borrowed French novels, German poetry and listened to operatic arias played on her neighbour's piano. She developed a deep love for the wild, open country and for the people who had come to settle it but her feelings about it were ambivalent. Because she grew up in a crude frontier society, she suffered for many years from a sense of cultural inferiority, describing herself disparagingly as a roughneck and envying those who came from older and superior civilisations.[7]

The years Cather spent at Lincoln State University (1890–95) were tremendously active and turbulent. Lincoln was a thriving city and railroad centre which, though it had only sprung into existence in 1867, already had schools, hotels and two large theatres by the time Cather enrolled at college. She arrived with the intention of becoming a doctor but an essay she wrote on Thomas Carlyle was printed in the Nebraska State *Journal* and, she claimed later, she was so affected by the sight of herself in print, she decided to become an author.[8] Apart from her course work, which included not only classes in English literature but the Classics, she edited the University literary magazine and began writing fiction. In 1893 she became the *Journal's* drama critic and Sunday columnist and rapidly developed a distinctive journalistic style. The paper's editor recalled that her reviews were of 'such biting frankness that . . . many an actor of national reputation wondered on coming to Lincoln what would appear the next morning from the pen of that meatax young girl of whom all of them had heard.'[9] Later, by working for the Lincoln *Courier* as well, she was able to be largely self-supporting. Her prodigious output of book and play reviews provides a fascinating record of her early artistic development and reveals how she was particularly drawn to late nineteenth-century European literature: the works of Carlyle, Ruskin, Maupassant, Alphonse Daudet, Pierre Loti, Flaubert, Tolstoy and Turgenev.

Cather's success in journalism while still a student was a considerable achievement but, despite the excitements of city and university life, this was not an altogether happy time. She wrote later that there are young people who can be themselves, simply and unaffectedly, but she had not been one of them.[10] She was eccentric in appearance and behaviour; she wore masculine clothing and closely cropped hair and was tactless and outspoken. Although she made a few good friends in Lincoln, as in Red Cloud, who remained loyal to her throughout her life, she was disliked and ridiculed by many. Again, it was among the European families that Cather was most at home but Lincoln society in general found William Cather Jr, as she called herself, hard to take. She soon found herself in the middle of a furore. It is difficult to piece together exactly what happened but from her letters it would seem that she fell in love with a student called Louise Pound. She sent Louise poems, rhapsodised over her dresses, railed at her other friends (male and female), and begged for photographs. She despaired that feminine friendship should be considered unnatural and was troubled that Louise might be disgusted by a good-night kiss. The letters are passionate, pleading, jealous and possessive.[11]

What happened in the end is not clear. It has been suggested that they fell out because Cather printed a satirical portrait of Louise's brother in the University magazine. Whatever the truth may have been, the episode was an unpleasant one. After Cather had graduated and moved to Pittsburgh (in 1896), to become editor of the *Home Monthly*, she wrote to her old friend Mariel Gere of how relieved she was to be beginning a new life in broad daylight away from the old mistakes. Without Mariel's help, she confessed, she never would have got through the Pound scrape but in Pittsburgh, without short hair or any other thing to queer her, she was delighted to find herself popular for the first time. She was invited to join all the women's clubs, and was full of the parties and picnics to which she had been. The magazine was trash but she earned enough to go to the opera and do as she liked. She was writing stories and had devoted herself to the worship of art, she wrote to Mariel, and if she became a success it would do her wicked heart good to pay off the old scores and make people take back the bitter things they had said.[12]

Cather's outward conformity and her obsession with privacy probably stem from a determination never to be exposed and hurt in the same way again. In later life her appearance was always impeccably correct and she never allowed her personal life to be commented on in public. But her brief adoption of a masculine identity raises interesting questions. Biographers have usually assumed, tacitly, that this stemmed from her homosexuality; that she wanted to assume a male role because of her attraction to other women. Although her earliest biographers skirt around the issue, the implication of lesbianism is always there and has led to some damaging and confused assumptions about her work. It has been inferred by several male critics, for example, that she could not write reliably about heterosexual relations because of her personal eccentricity.[13]

More recent, feminist criticism has at least dispensed with euphemism and innuendo and tried to tackle the question openly.[14] However, it is difficult to be conclusive. Collections of her letters show that her enduring friendships were almost exclusively with women but as there is hardly any surviving correspondence with Isabelle McClung and Edith Lewis, the two most important women in her life, it is not clear whether her feeling for either of them was sexual or not.[15] The very fact that she had her letters to them destroyed, and that Lewis never once went home to Red Cloud with her, are probable indications. On the other hand, Cather received two proposals of marriage during her twenties, which she apparently seriously considered, and in 1912, while on holiday in the Southwest, she met a Mexican named Julio about whose masculine charms she wrote several pages of fulsome appreciation to her friend Elizabeth Sergeant.[16]

Although Cather never mentions the subject in print, there are very scathing references to homosexuals in her private letters. She was, for example, absolutely furious when approached for her memories of A. E. Housman by some young men – willie boys, as she called them – who had sent her their manuscripts and intended, according to Cather, to impute their own effeminacy to Housman, the scholar and gentleman. Were they hypnotised by the word, 'lad'? She defended Housman's "heterosexuality" as if her life depended on it.[17] But whether Cather was, in fact, a lesbian or not is unlikely to be conclusively established one way or the other. More fruitfully, feminist critics have turned from speculation about sexual preference and begun to examine the social implications of Cather's male identification. Sharon O'Brien, for example, explores the problems Cather faced as a young woman wanting to become a writer; her attempt 'to fashion a female self that could be compatible with the artist's role' when there were 'no acceptable models for identity and vocation in the late-Victorian culture.'[18]

This was an issue which certainly did preoccupy Cather. In her vast output of journalism, between 1893 and 1902, there are several discussions of the rival claims of marriage and a career and assessments of women artists. These articles, the product of youth and haste, full of rhetoric, high spirits and bombast, give a vivid impression of Cather's mental climate during this period. They make it abundantly clear that she was no feminist: if it was difficult for women to achieve anything outside the domestic sphere, she was inclined to believe it was their own fault. 'I have not much faith in women in fiction', she confessed in 1895: 'They have a sort of sex consciousness that is abominable. They are so limited to one string and they so lie about that.' She could admire only Miss Brontë (she does not say which), Jane Austen, George Eliot and George Sand. Moreover, in her eyes the 'two great Georges' were 'anything but women'. Her disgust with romantic fiction is understandable, if a little excessive; she felt it had become difficult to take women writers seriously because of the plethora of what George Eliot called, 'silly novels by lady novelists'. Full of lordly disdain, Cather shook her head at their feeble efforts: 'Women are so horribly subjective and they have such scorn for the healthy commonplace. When a woman writes a story of adventure, a stout sea tale, a manly battle yarn, anything without wine, women and love, then I will begin to hope for something great for them, not before.'[19]

Born in the late nineteenth century, in a society which accepted the secondary status of women, Cather swallowed the notion of male supremacy whole. Later she outgrew the simplistic equation of maleness with greatness, but in her youth the culture she admired was dominated by men – Wagner, Tolstoy, Flaubert – and she was loath to identify herself with the weaker vessels. Mercifully, Cather spared us the stout sea tale and the manly battle yarn, realising that her way forward did not lie in pretending to be a man, but in rejecting sexual stereotypes altogether. She did not perpetrate a masculine imitation but developed an individual voice that refused to be confined to the conventional, feminine sphere. She grew less afraid of the 'abominable' sex consciousness but throughout her life she remained acutely aware of the disadvantages of being classified as a Lady Author.[20]

Sometime in 1899, while working for the Pittsburgh *Leader*, Cather met Isabelle McClung. She was wealthy and beautiful, shared Cather's interest in theatre and music, and encouraged her to write. In 1901, after working as a freelance journalist in Washington, Cather moved in with Isabelle and her parents and for the next five years taught English at the Central and Allegheny High Schools. With long holidays and no domestic worries Cather had more time for her own work. It seems to have been a settled and happy period: she enjoyed teaching, she visited Europe for the first time, and published a slim volume of verse, *April Twilights* (1903), and a collection of short stories, *The Troll Garden* (1905). Although she had poked fun at stuffy Presbyterians when she first moved to Pittsburgh, she seems to have been at ease in Judge McClung's solidly bourgeois household and, even after she moved to New York, often returned to the study Isabelle had arranged for her in the attic, in order to write.

Working for *McClure's Magazine* was a mixed blessing. It enabled her to move (in 1906) to New York, America's literary centre, and the job was exciting. The magazine published stories by Kipling, Stevenson, Hardy, Arnold Bennett, Stephen Crane, London, Conan Doyle and Twain. S.S. McClure reckoned he lost more money publishing Conrad than anyone else alive. But *McClure's* was also famous for its muckraking and Cather, who had no interest in social reform, came to resent devoting so much of her energy to editing poorly written articles on government swindles and slum housing. At first she was delighted to be visiting the Metropolitan opera, meeting artists and musicians; there were trips to Europe and she was devoted to McClure, but after five years she was dismayed at how little she had managed to achieve as a writer.

It was on one of her muckraking expeditions for McClure that Cather met the New England writer Sarah Orne Jewett. She, and her friend Mrs Fields, were part of Boston's intellectual élite and Cather was flattered to be admitted

into their circle. Jewett became an important influence on
her; advising her to give up journalism and concentrate
on her own work. Cather had never, even in her youth,
considered the possibility of running off and writing a
novel, trusting to talent and good luck, and even in her
mature years her insecurity was acute. The letters she wrote
to Jewett show Cather almost on her knees to the Dear
Lady, as she called her, pleading for her approval.[21] In
the author of *The Country of the Pointed Firs*, Cather found
a contemporary woman writer whom she could admire. But
despite Jewett's encouragement, Cather was nearly forty
years old before she finally left the magazine.

With the critical acclaim of *Alexander's Bridge* (1912),
Cather grew more confident and from then on was able
to give up journalism and maintain herself, in relative
comfort, on the proceeds of her writing. She followed
Jewett's suggestion that she should write about her own
country and in 1913 published *O Pioneers!*, the first of her
Western novels. For as long as the family home remained,
Cather kept returning to Red Cloud. Her attachment to
the place was so strong that she was even tempted at
one time to 'settle down on a quarter section of land
and let [her] writing go.' But when she was actually
there, the immensity and emptiness of the prairie made
her terrified of 'dying in a cornfield' and she longed to
return to the Atlantic coast, where she was 'surrounded by
the great masters and teachers with all their tradition and
learning and culture'.[22] Cather never found an ideal home
but she remained, somewhat uneasily, in New York.

It was here that she met Edith Lewis, with whom
she shared an apartment until she died. Although Phyllis
Robinson states that their 'life together was undoubtedly
a marriage in every sense', there is no concrete evidence to support this.[23] Biographers have tended rather
to ignore Lewis, prompted, perhaps, by a desire for tidi-
ness; McClung is invariably portrayed as the big romance

in Cather's life, with Lewis as the loyal but less than scintillating companion. This is very probably a gross simplification. Judging from the book she wrote about Cather, Lewis must have been an intelligent and cultured woman but so little given to self-advertisement that it is difficult to gain a picture of her. The one letter from Cather to Lewis which somehow escaped destruction is intimate and tender. None the less, Isabelle McClung's marriage in 1916 came as a terrible blow, despite the fact that Cather and Lewis had already been living together for about eight years. When Isabelle died in 1938, Cather wrote to a friend that she thought most novelists wrote for one person and for her that person had been Isabelle.[24]

With the appearance of *The Song of the Lark* (1915), which is dedicated to Isabelle, the period of Cather's greatest creativity begins. Novels such as *My Ántonia* (1918) and the Pulitzer Prize-winning *One of Ours* (1922), were so successful that she could afford to turn down munificent offers from Hollywood and never had to compromise her integrity by writing potboilers, or having her work anthologised in cheap 'omnibus' editions. Once she had overcome her initial hesitancy she wrote to please herself, ignoring critical and literary fashions and relying on her own instincts as an artist. This made her a somewhat isolated figure. She was particularly out of sympathy with the novel of social criticism and voiced her objections uncompromisingly on several occasions.[25] From her youth to her death she never wavered in her conviction that 'economics and art are strangers'. She could not believe that society would ever be changed by a novel: reformers should confine themselves to pamphleteering and artists should devote themselves to the enduring human values and emotions. American writers, from Hamlin Garland to Theodore Dreiser and Dos Passos, who espoused theories or amassed documentary fact, were of no interest to her.

The American avant-garde did not impress her greatly. She had no time for Ezra Pound and Amy Lowell: poems about 'wet oyster shell[s]' against 'wet beach[es]' left her cold. And according to Sergeant she found the self-styled mother of American literature, Gertrude Stein, too absurd to even discuss.[26] But, although she inveighed against waywardness and assaults upon punctuation, this was not due to any reverence for convention – she had, after all, published free verse herself in *April Twilights* (1903). She believed in experimentation; that writers cannot simply adhere 'to the old patterns' but must search 'for something new and untried.'[27] But what she found in the majority of her compatriots was at best merely lively reportage and at worst superficial novelty. She particularly admired Thorton Wilder and Scott Fitzgerald and had ambivalent feelings about Sinclair Lewis.[28] Her favourite contemporary American poet was Robert Frost. The relative silence on the subject of Cather's work suggests that the contempt she felt for the majority of her fellows was mutual. None the less, when Sinclair Lewis received the Nobel Prize in 1930, he was reported to have said that Miss Cather should have had it; Faulkner paid her the backhanded compliment of remarking that not even Willa Cather could convince him a woman could write; Fitzgerald was worried that he had unconsciously plagiarised from her, and Wallace Stevens considered that 'we have nothing better than she is'.[29]

In the larger context of literature written in English she is often seen as something of an anachronism in the age which saw the proliferation of such experimental novelists as James Joyce, Virginia Woolf and D. H. Lawrence. Cather apparently considered *Ulysses* to be a 'landmark' and respected Virginia Woolf, but one can only assume that her interest in both of them was of a fairly desultory kind, as there is not a mention of any of their books in her critical writings or letters.[30] As for Lawrence, though she liked him as a man, he is summarily dismissed in 'The Novel Démeublé': 'Can anyone imagine anything more terrible than the story of Romeo and Juliet rewritten in prose by D. H. Lawrence?'[31] Characteristically, her evaluation of *The Rainbow* depends on a humanist and artistic disapproval of Lawrence's tendency to treat emotions as mere sensory reactions. Whatever technical innovations he may have introduced in the novel, to Cather his 'laboratory study of bodily organs under sensory stimuli' harked back to nineteenth-century Naturalism. But she admired Katherine Mansfield, Thomas Mann and Joseph Conrad.[32] Clearly she was not, as has been suggested, completely estranged from the Modern Movement.

Cather is invariably portrayed as having no coterie and leaving no disciples. None the less, she was not such an isolated figure as she appears today. She had friends who were writers, with whom she discussed work, but they were all women and have been largely forgotten. With the three most important of these she maintained a lifelong correspondence: the novelist Dorothy Canfield, whom she met at University; the playwright Zoë Akins, and the novelist and essayist Elizabeth Sergeant, both of whom were friends from the *McClure* days. She was fond of the poet Sara Teasdale, and in later life met Sigrid Undset and became a great admirer of Undset's Norwegian epics. There was no question of a shared literary manifesto. Indeed, there was considerable disagreement at times; Cather felt that Sergeant wasted time on politics that should have been spent on her work, and was upset by Akin's play *Starvation on Red River*, which she found forced and improbable. But between Cather and each of these writers there was plenty of lively debate and, above all, tremendous loyalty and affection.

Most of Cather's maturity was devoted to writing. She lived for the most part in New York but often escaped from it. She spent summers in Jaffrey, New Hampshire (where she was buried), and on Grand Manan Island, New Brunswick, which she loved for the peace and beauty of

its woods and streams and cliff walks. She made trips to
Europe, and also spent long vacations in the Southwest and
later in Quebec. Her outward life was largely uneventful:
she wrote, travelled, listened to music and saw her friends.
She was not a recluse, as has so often been stated; she
simply refused to become a personage. Once she became
famous she found she had to barricade herself against the
incessant demands to lecture, give readings and interviews,
join literary clubs and attend literary luncheons. For her,
all this had nothing to do with literature. Ironically, by
trying to avoid public attention, she became a myth and
she lived to grow heartily sick of the legend of herself as
a pale creature who had sacrificed everything to her art.[33]

Her last years, though, grew increasingly bleak. She suffered from minor illnesses and injuries to her hands which
made writing difficult. It seemed to her that it simply rained
death: both her parents, her brothers Douglas and Roscoe to
whom she had been closest, Isabelle McClung and other old
friends, all died. She grew disenchanted with many aspects
of contemporary life and despaired at the increasing tide of
commercialisation and mass production. She lived through
a time of considerable upheaval: the First World War,
the advent of the automobile and moving pictures, the
rise of America's vast, sprawling cities and tremendous
changes in social attitudes and manners. The outbreak
of the Second World War heralded to her the end of
everything she had cherished and with the fall of Paris
she wrote in her line-a-day diary: 'There seems to be
no hope at all for people of my generation.'[34]

Cather never became a bitter old woman but the occasional flashes of anger and despair which escaped her have
earned her that reputation. The most notorious of these
outbursts occurs in the preface to her collection of essays,
Not Under Forty (1936), in which she informs her readers
that if they have not attained the required age they need
read no further; the book 'is for the backward and by one of

their number'. Cather's truculence was, in part, provoked: she herself had been attacked by Marxist critics and, as a private letter makes plain, certain graduates of New York University had been delving into Sarah Orne Jewett's private life and discussing 'sex starvation' amongst provincial ladies. Cather was outraged and her essay on Jewett, although it never addresses the issue of Jewett's sexuality directly, was clearly prompted by a passionate desire to defend her early mentor's reputation. Later she changed the title and omitted the preface but the damage was done: she stood convicted of nostalgia and conservatism.[35]

When Cather moved into her Park Avenue apartment in 1932 it signalled to many that she had become an established figure. Elizabeth Sergeant, for example, wondered whether Neighbour Rosicky or Grandma Harris could have got past the porter; with the implication that Cather had somehow betrayed her allegiance to the immigrants and unpretentious country people. But she chose her address for its seclusion, not its social cachet. Sergeant also shows Cather as having all the brutal indifference of the self-made woman: 'Nobody, young people especially, should be helped; no artist or writer either. Endowments, frescoes for public buildings, travelling fellowships be damned.' But all through the Depression, Cather sent a succession of cheques to farming families in Nebraska, to help them buy seed and meet mortgage payments, and serialised *Lucy Gayheart* in order to be able to do so. She also contributed in secret to a fund for the impoverished S. S. McClure.[36]

Cather's feeling for life was intense and, in unguarded moments, she expressed her views in an extreme form. She admitted to a friend that she always wanted to hang garlands on people or put them to torture.[37] Neither her political opinions nor her attitude to literature stemmed from a systematised philosophy: she responded to an event individually, often emotionally. It was because of this that she was so reluctant to expound her views in print: she did

not want to be committed to opinions she had held ten years
before. However, it is not as a critic or thinker that she is
important and in her novels, her opinions and prejudices
of the moment fall away and become irrelevant. She never
began a creative work from an immediate impression, or
in the heat of reaction, but followed Sarah Orne Jewett's
advice: 'find your own quiet centre of life and write from
that'.[38] Her greatest books are the fruit of long and calm
reflection, and of profound sympathy, which perhaps
because it cost her so much, is all the more convincing.

Many reminiscences of the elderly Cather show an
austere, almost patrician figure. Robert Frost's verdict
is fairly typical: 'With Willa Cather, it was "the people,
no."' Even Yehudi Menuhin, to whom Cather was like an
aunt, remembers her as all 'country tweediness', with more
than a hint of Christian Temperance about her.[39] But there
was another side to her character. In a recently discovered
collection of her letters to Stephen Tennant she is candid,
witty and generous. She encourages him in his work, laughs
at his youthful posturings and tells how she hid his, outra-
geous but delightful, *Leaves from a Missionary's Notebook* in
a locked drawer. Indeed, it is particularly unfortunate that
Cather forbade the publication of her letters because with
her relaxed, playful style with friends, her honesty and
concern, they are not only revealing, but very attractive.

Truman Capote's highly perceptive reminiscence also
shows a very different figure from the stereotype of the
elderly Cather as a withdrawn and forbidding spinster.
In his account she appears elegant, outgoing and amused.
Their unlikely friendship sprang from an encounter outside the New York Society Library in 1942 when Capote
was nineteen, and Cather, though she would probably
never have admitted it, nearly seventy:

Occasionally, I saw a woman there whose appearance
rather mesmerized me – her eyes especially: blue, the

pale brilliant cloudless blue of prairie skies. But even
without this singular feature, her face was interesting
– firm-jawed, handsome, a bit androgynous. Pepper-salt
hair parted in the middle. Sixty-five, thereabouts . . .

One January day I emerged from the library into
the twilight to find a heavy snowfall in progress. The
lady with the blue eyes, wearing a nicely cut black
coat with a sable collar, was waiting at the curb. A
gloved, taxi-summoning hand was poised in the air,
but there were no taxis. She looked at me and smiled
and said: 'Do you think a cup of hot chocolate would
help? There's a Longchamps around the corner.'

She ordered hot chocolate; I asked for a 'very' dry mar-
tini. Half seriously, she said, 'Are you old enough?'[40]

In the course of conversation he discovered, with a
'frisson', that she was the author of *My Ántonia, A Lost
Lady, The Professor's House*. They became friends; she read
his work and was always 'a fair and helpful judge'; 'a good
listener' and a 'crisply pointed' conversationalist. Capote
may not always be the most reliable witness but his portrait
seems to capture the spirit of Cather as it is manifest in her
books – warm, generous, with a quiet humour.

# 2 To Bayreuth and back again:

*The Troll Garden, The Song of the Lark, One of Ours, Uncle Valentine*

> "What a difference Wagner made in the world, after all,"
>
> Charlotte Waterford in *Uncle Valentine*

Picture a young woman in the early 1890s sitting in a cornfield howling because she cannot hear any music dramas. Give her all the music she wants, take her about the world a little until her mind finds what it is hunting for, and she will come out all right with the corn.[1] This is Cather's explanation of her early hostility to Nebraska and of her subsequent change of heart. All her dissatisfaction with the narrowness and philistinism of the American small town, and her impatience to be part of the great intellectual and artistic circles of her day, found expression in her passion for the music of Richard Wagner. From her vantage point in Red Cloud, Wagner represented the pinnacle of European culture and everything that America lacked. Paradoxically, it was the example of his work which led her home again, to the source of her creativity, by showing her the value of symbol and archetype. On the simplest level, as America had no cycle of legends of its own, she could always borrow his and write about Siegfrieds and Parsifals of the prairie, rainbow bridges over Chicago and Rhinegold in Pittsburgh. More profoundly, she learned from Wagner as the mythologist of national origins, discovering that America too had an ancient past and, if not a mythology, the stuff out of which myths are made.

Towards the end of her life Cather said that she had spent more time listening to music than most people spent on their careers: her enthusiasm began early and never diminished.[2] Even before Cather had been to a performance of Wagner, the cosmopolitan critic of the *Journal* did not let this inhibit her from referring to the Master as if she were a fully fledged *aficionado*. By March 1894 he was included in her pantheon of artistic heroes when she castigated the 'guild of drawing-room critics' who have 'declared Ruskin and Wagner and Turner and Modjeska blasé'. The 'parlour critics' found Wagner 'overdrawn, coarse, stagey, unnatural' but Cather, revelling in Romantic rebellion, threw down her gauntlet: 'Make your own world as moderate and proper and conventional as you wish, but behind the footlights let people love with kisses and suffer with tears.'[3]

Her apparently gratuitous idolisation is not as surprising as it seems at first. Bryan Magee in *Aspects of Wagner* concluded that 'Wagner has had a greater influence than any other single artist on the culture of our age.'[4] Many writers felt his impact before they ever heard the music; Raymond Furness in *Wagner and Literature* recounts how C. S. Lewis 'experienced the very shape of his name as a magic symbol' and how Lord Berners, merely glimpsing the score of *Das Rheingold* in a shop window, felt like Dante when he first saw Beatrice on the bridge in Florence.[5] There have been several accounts of Wagner's profound and varied influence on English and European literature but American authors seem to have been considerably less impressed. The journey from Germany through Symboliste France, to Edwardian England and Ireland, has been well documented but somehow Wagner also made his way to Cather perched, as Ford Maddox Ford liked to think of her, on her slag heap in Pittsburgh.

Cather was not only unique amongst Americans in her debt to Wagner but decidedly original in her response. Wagnerism reached epidemic proportions in Europe and Cather was not entirely in accord with all its manifestations. The quasi-religious element in his work, or rather the attempt of some of his acolytes to extrapolate from this a Wagnerian metaphysic, struck her as being invariably 'pretentious' and 'stupid'. She was not a Perfect Wagnerite either. Although she did not demur from Shaw's social and political analysis of the *Ring*, she was not very interested in it. In her review of *The Perfect Wagnerite* she concluded that Shaw would 'naturally' regard Wotan as a symbol of obsolescent government but that 'Mr. Shaw's volume is scarcely satisfactory on the strong love theme in the *Ring*, which after all concerned Wagner much more nearly than the perplexities of his gods.'[6]

Wagner's appeal for Cather was not as a philosopher but as an artist. The music dramas were first and foremost Romances; stories of human emotion in a heightened form. She delighted in the legendary atmosphere, in *Lohengrin* as 'a radiant incarnation of youth and chivalry' but above all she gloried in the portrayal of passion. She 'read' the operas as if they were works of literature. In 1899 she had never heard a performance of *Tristan and Isolde* but she was alive to what she later called Wagner's 'rough' poetry; 'the sting of the potion' on Isolde's lips and 'the waves that lash so madly on the Irish coast'. Her reviews all focus on drama and characterisation. In the *Ring* Cather found essential and universal truths of human experience, 'the inexplicable law that tires out even the hearts of the gods, that binds and fetters in Valhalla just as it does in Pittsburgh or in Lincoln.[7]

In her preface to Gertrude Hall's *Wagnerian Romances* (1925) Cather offers her most explicit statement of Wagner's attraction:

But opera is a hybrid art, – part literary to begin with. It happens that in Wagnerian music drama the literary part of the work is not trivial, as it so often is in operas, but is truly the mate of the music, done by the same hand. The music is throughout concerned with words, and with things that can be presented in language; with human beings and their passions and sorrows . . .[8]

Like many writers before her, Cather was dismayed at 'entrancing arias' being sung to 'insincere and grotesque plots'.[9] Wagner's doctrine of the *Gesamtkünstwerk*, of every element contributing to the sense of dramatic coherency, made opera a potent force in literature for the first time.

In her review of *Lohengrin* in 1899 Cather discusses one of the aspects of Wagnerism which most influenced her own work. She cites the knight's appeal to Elsa in the third act not to seek his identity: it is a lesson to 'every analytical student' in the futility of 'killing a flower to find its name'. Although she began as a staunch advocate of scientific investigation – her High School Commencement Speech had pleaded the cause of vivisection – she rapidly lost faith in it. Perhaps Wagner, a passionate anti-vivisectionist, was instrumental in her conversion. Certainly his belief that, as she phrased it, 'too much analysis destroys',[10] had a profound and lasting effect. Orthodox interpretations of *Lohengrin* stress the conflict between Christian and pagan values but to Cather the dramatic tension lay in the opposition of the rational and the Romantic. It is the compulsion to 'construct systems' which brings about 'poor practical' Elsa's downfall.

The antithesis between poetic truth and empirical truth became a dominant theme in her work. Moreover, it is related to the structure of the novels themselves. She rejected the plot-dominated novels which had been the staple of the nineteenth century and allowed her material to find its own form. The novelistic process, as is evident if one compares

*Alexander's Bridge* (1912) with *O Pioneers!* (1913), became not a question of intellectual arrangements of interesting subject matter but a natural development whereby characters and events settled into their inevitable places. The former, she said, followed a 'conventional pattern' but in the latter there was no '"inventing"; everything was spontaneous and took its own place, right or wrong.'[11] Here one can see a strong parallel with Wagner, who ignored the prevailing operatic trappings of mistaken identities, sub-plots and contrived denouements, and opted for a principle of organic growth.

At first sight it might seem mistaken to relate the author of 'The Novel Démeublé' to Wagner and his large-scale, even grandiose compositions but at this stage Cather had not yet formulated her theory of the art of suggestion and was more excited by the big effect than by delicacy or precision. She was eager to impress: in her juvenilia she had attempted to write about the Midwest but as the material seemed unpromising she turned her attention to what she considered to be more acceptable literary subjects. Her first volume of stories, *The Troll Garden* (1905), is the fruit of this.[12] It deals exclusively with artists: creative and performing artists, the failed and successful, spurious and genuine. The major themes are the interaction of life and art and the hostility of Philistia (relocated in America) to real endeavour. She focuses particularly on the woman artist; the tensions involved in pursuing a career and having a family or the stark option of choosing between the two.

One of the most bleak yet profound of these explorations is 'A Wagner Matinee' – which is also the clearest expression of the opposition in Cather's mind between Wagner, the apogee of civilisation, and the cultural wasteland of Nebraska. In it the elderly Georgina Carpenter returns to Boston to visit her nephew after spending most of her adult life on a Midwestern farm. She had studied the piano in her youth, in Boston and Paris, but had given up the possibility of a career when she married and moved West. Her nephew Clark, the narrator, takes her to an afternoon concert and as she hears Wagner's music again, for the first time in thirty years, she is filled with a sickening sense of loss.

Georgina Carpenter is too downtrodden to rebel against her position or articulate her despair; it is only guessed at by the narrator as he watches her listen. The first half of the programme comprises the overtures to *Tannhauser* and *The Flying Dutchman*, the prelude to *Tristan and Isolde* and the 'Prize Song' from *The Mastersingers*. In the second half there are some unspecified numbers from the *Ring*, culminating with Siegfried's Funeral March. The tragedy of Aunt Georgina's life is revealed through her response to the music: 'Soon after the tenor began the Prize Song, I heard a quick drawn breath and turned to my aunt. Her eyes were closed, but the tears were glistening on her cheeks'. And the musical themes underline her tragedy: the conflict between the Pilgrim and Venusberg motifs in *Tannhauser* and the Senta and Curse motifs in *The Flying Dutchman* both emphasise the conflict in Georgina Carpenter between music and marriage.

Cather's use of Wagner is impressionistic and there is no need, as Richard Giannone does, to enforce any strict parallels.[13] According to Giannone, for example, the 'Pilgrims' Chorus' 'represents the higher impulses of Georgina Carpenter' while the Venusberg motif represents the 'tempting world created of man's profane desires' – in her case 'the arid plains of Red Willow county.' Indeed, nearly all the items on the programme are about 'the war between man's higher and lower instincts' and serve as 'ironic comments on Aunt Georgina's defeat'. However, the inclusion of the 'Prize Song', which celebrates the 'triumph of art and life', surely answers the contending themes in *Tannhauser* and *The Flying Dutchman* and suggests that it is possible to be a married artist. In any case Aunt Georgina hardly deserves such a relentless ironic commentary.

The allusions to Wagner evoke the world that she has lost but they are not intended as moral comments. *Tannhauser* is anything but a musical sermon and, as Cather said in her review, it is precisely because the claims of sacred and profane love are of equal weight 'that the opera derives [its] meaning and power.'[14] Georgina Carpenter's tragedy is not so much that she fell in love – that there was, in Giannone's terms, 'no victory for the higher yearnings' – but that she ended up in Nebraska. By no stretch of the imagination could Cather have expected the farm to function as a parallel to the 'sensous splendour of Venusberg'. Here it is in Clark's memory:

> I saw again the tall, naked house on the prairie, black and grim as a wooden fortress; the black pond where I had learned to swim, its margin pitted with sun-dried cattle tracks; the rain gullied clay banks about the naked house . . .

Only a masochist would have been 'tempted' by that.

Aunt Georgina's deprivation is evoked with dramatic immediacy at the end of the concert: 'The harpist slipped its green felt cover over his instrument; the flute-players shook the water from their mouthpieces; the men of the orchestra went out one by one, leaving the stage to the chairs and the music stands, empty as a winter cornfield.' Cather deftly fuses her descriptions so that one world comments on the other. The flat monotony of the plains, 'where, as in a treadmill, one might walk from daybreak to dusk without perceiving a shadow of change' contrasts with the landscape of the orchestra: 'the beloved shapes of the instruments, the patches of yellow light thrown by the green shaded lamps on the smooth, varnished bellies of the 'cellos and the bass viols in the rear, the restless, wind-tossed forest of fiddle necks and bows.'

Contemplating his aunt, Clark wonders, 'Had this music any message for her?' As she sits silently weeping he imagines that it takes her on a sea journey, which in this context inevitably summons *Tristan and Isolde* to mind:

> The deluge of sound poured on and on; I never knew what she found in the shining current of it; . . . From the trembling of her face I could well believe that before the last numbers she had been carried out where the myriad graves are, into the grey, nameless burying grounds of the sea; or into some world of death vaster yet, where, from the beginning of the world, hope has lain down with hope and dream with dream and, renouncing, slept.

The melody which Isolde hears takes her too on a voyage towards death. As Clark imagines Aunt Georgina drowning in the deluge of sound, the passage, with its surging rhythm, becomes her 'Liebestod'. Like Isolde she is defeated by social and physical reality but both transcend the limitations of this world, and through renunciation, sail towards a more complete fulfilment. Before she can be transported to this 'world of death' she has to face again the barren landscape of Nebraska:

> For her, just outside the door of the concert hall, lay the black pond with the cattle-tracked bluffs; the tall, unpainted house, the weather-curled boards; naked as a tower, the crook-backed ash seedlings where the dishcloths hung to dry; the gaunt, moulting turkeys picking up refuse about the kitchen door.

The ash seedling are perhaps intended to recall the great ash tree in *Die Walküre*, from which *Nothung* springs, but in 'A Wagner matinee' they sprout only dishcloths in a devastating image of domestic dreariness.

Other stories in *The Troll Garden* draw on Wagnerian music drama but none so successfully as 'A Wagner

Matinee'. 'The Garden Lodge', for example, which also concerns a failed woman artist, is a contemporary reworking of Act I of *Die Walküre*. Caroline Noble, who comes from a penniless family of artists, was not forced to give up her career; she refused the struggle to become a concert pianist, took refuge in a companionable marriage to Howard Noble, a wealthy Wall Street broker, and exchanged squalor for security. Prompted by her husband's suggestion that they should pull down the old garden lodge, which had been the scene of her flirtation with the Wagnerian tenor, d'Esquerré, she begins to have regrets.

In Cather's version, Caroline plays Sieglinde, Howard a civilised Hunding, d'Esquerré is Siegmund and the lodge is Hunding's hut. Most of the story is a flashback to the time when d'Esquerré, weary from his battles in the opera world, arrived at the Nobles' to find the beautiful Caroline ready to restore him. She recalls how they had been playing over the first act of *Die Walküre*, d'Esquerré had led her from the keyboard, and as he sang 'Thou art the Spring for which I sighed in Winter's cold embraces' she had felt 'the whisper of a question from the hand under her heart'. (In fact this is Sieglinde's line but it is obviously more convenient to have the tenor do the singing!) In the transposition of the *Volsung* legend into a modern, bourgeois setting, the story gains considerable ironic thrust. The Wagnerian duo's passionate declaration of mutual love is here only a hesitant possibility; she retained 'her self-control' and 'he had seemed to take for granted' that she would. Caroline becomes Sieglinde only in her dream. In the morning she is humiliated by her erotic fantasy, and announces her decision to have the lodge destroyed, but not without a sense of loss and the awareness that 'this happy, useful, well-ordered life was not enough'.

'The Garden Lodge' is skilful but somewhat self-conscious. In this it is representative of the faults of *The Troll Garden* as a whole which, as the fruit of Cather's friendships with opera singers and artists, and her excitement at becoming part of the world of culture and ideas, rarely manages to rise above the level of extremely lively reportage. The best of the collection, 'A Sculptor's Funeral', 'Paul's Case' and 'A Wagner Matinee', explore the same themes but because they contain a measure of felt experience, they are not so circumscribed by artificiality and contrivance. 'Paul's Case', for example, concerns a young boy of artistic temperament but no talent, overwhelmed by the ugliness and mundanity of Pittsburgh's suburbia, who steals from his employer and spends a few glorious days of splendour and luxury in New York before committing suicide. Although the story was based on a newspaper report, Paul's case was similar to Cather's own, with the important exception that hers was redeemed by a dedication to writing.

Her next book was *Alexander's Bridge* (1912), an account of an engineer's infatuation with an actress, followed by *O Pioneers!* (1913) in which she returned to the immigrant farmers of the Midwest in an attempt, perhaps, to escape from the artificiality which the subject matter of *The Troll Garden* and *Alexander's Bridge* had seemed to necessitate. The number of commentaries on the ordering of the stories within the collection testifies to that element of 'arrangement' which she came to think of as the hallmark of the second rate and she thought so poorly of the novel that she did not want it republished. But the story of an opera singer growing up in the Midwest promised the best of both worlds and, with Wagner's example of organic design, it could unfold with a naturalness that accounts of artistic development had often failed to achieve. Significantly, it was not until Cather accepted her native land as a valid subject for art that she portrayed a successful artist. *The Song of the Lark* (1915) is the first of Cather's works to use Wagner, not as a way of rubbing America's nose in its philistinism, but as a means to creating its own art forms and appreciating those it already had.

In what sense is *The Song of the Lark* a Wagnerian novel?

It is certainly not 'a symphony in full stops and commas', as Moore described Dujardin's *Les Lauriers sont Coupés* (1888).[15] Cather never attempted a full-scale application of Wagnerian technique to prose as Dujardin, and Moore in *The Lake* (1905), had done. She was eager to learn from music but was well aware of the special limitations and possibilities of each form. Moore's experiments with the 'unending melody' of narrative prompted Wilde to remark that he had heard one of Moore's novels was to be played on the piano! Cather never tried to stretch the boundaries of prose narrative in this way. *The Song of the Lark* is a *Bildungsroman*, giving the growing awareness of the central character and the influence of the environment. She took from Wagner only those features most readily adaptable to literature. For example, Thea Kronburg's growth of consciousness is charted by leitmotif, as memories of the past surface at each stage of her development. Less directly musical is Cather's debt to Wagner as the mythologist of national origins: Thea's artistic coming of age occurs at Panther Cañon with the discovery that the Ancient People had lengthened her past and given her 'older and higher obligations' (383). Cather also found in Wagner a rich mine of symbol and analogue.

A comparison with George Moore's *Evelyn Innes* (1898) – the European novel of a Wagnerian soprano – reveals much about Cather's process and highlights her distinctive use of Wagner. Apart from Henry James, she found that most writers digressed interminably when they attempted to portray the life of an artist: George Sand in *Consuelo* (1842) and Mrs Humphrey Ward in *Miss Bretherton* (1884) were among the worst offenders. But she spoke glowingly of Moore's novel on several occasions: it is a 'searching and sympathetic study of the artistic temperament'; 'an admirably constructed' book, 'in which nothing superfluous is tolerated, and in which all the incidental philosophising and moralising is made to support and strengthen the story proper'.[16]

Moore achieves this sense of unity by making Evelyn's life parallel those of the Wagnerian heroines she plays on stage. This not only justifies the fairly lengthy discussion of Wagner's work but provides Moore with a fertile source of comparison. Indeed, art and life become almost indistinguishable at times. When Evelyn returns to London to beg forgiveness from her estranged father (for having run away with her lover, Owen Asher) she is conscious of playing Brünnhilde to his Wotan. She can barely distinguish between the third act of *Die Walküre* and reality: Brünnhilde's words 'broke from her lips' and she 'heard the swelling harmony, every chord'.[17] Cather never makes so close an identification and such parallels as do exist are only suggested obliquely.

In *Evelyn Innes* art comments on life and life on art. Evelyn's personal experience informs her interpretations; her compelling account of Elisabeth's renunciation in *Tannhauser*, for example, is drawn from memories of her cloistered youth. Evelyn is a lapsed Catholic who has led an irregular life but on stage she is again 'a virgin whose sole reality has been her father and her châtelaine' (188). Thea, too, identifies with and illuminates the roles she plays. Her Elisabeth, of course, has a different provenance – Moonstone rather than Dulwich – and gains a different interpretation. Her accompanist, Landry, observes that she was working on the part during her mother's illness: '"[It] might be any lonely woman getting ready to die"' (540). Both Moore and Cather emphasise the essential truth of Wagner's vision but Moore concentrates on, and to some extent is confined by, the 'truth' of sexuality. Characteristically, Evelyn's Elisabeth is a virgin, Thea's is 'any lonely woman'.

The nineteenth-century assumption that women who appeared on stage, exposing themselves to the public, must therefore be immodest if not immoral, hovers in the background of Evelyn's career. Although Moore does not condemn his heroine he evidently still harbours a suspicion that as she is a performer she is unlikely to be a prude. Cather brushes the whole misconception aside. Thea, unusually for actresses in literature, is not even conventionally beautiful. And, whereas Moore's novel opens with Evelyn about to begin her career, Cather spends over a third of hers on Thea's childhood. Her main interest is not in the problems facing an actress but the making of an artist.

Evelyn is consistently identified with Isolde and her interpretation of the role is animated by a sensuality which is yet further inflamed by the passion of Wagner's music. After a performance of *Tristan* she 'loosed the hand of her stage lover' and threw herself into the arms of Ulick Dean murmuring, much to the reader's embarrassment, '"That music maddens me"' (291–292). Towards the end of the novel it is suggested that she should play Kundry – the guilt-ridden temptress who finds redemption in drying Parsifal's feet with her hair – but significantly she retires to a nunnery instead. To be fair to Moore, he never posits renunciation as a satisfactory solution to the vexed question of female sexuality. In contrast, though Thea is the daughter of a Methodist minister, she is singularly untroubled by religious doubts or strictures – she leaves the latter to her pious sister Anna. The full force of her energy is channelled into becoming a singer and it is through art that she finds fulfilment, without any need of religion.

Although there are superficial similarities, Cather's treatment of sexuality is also very different. Fred Ottenburg is the counterpart to Owen Asher: both are rich men of the world and musical amateurs who promote the careers of their chosen divas. The contrast in attitude between the two authors emerges most clearly in the courtship scenes. Wagner provides the catalyst for Moore's pair when Owen plays 'the love music out of "Tristan" on the harpsichord' (73). Within minutes of this bizarre serenade they are planning to elope to Paris. Fred, too, releases his lover from the bondage of music lessons with a kiss but their background music is Grieg's 'Tak for dit Räd', which Thea translates as '"Thanks for your advice! But I prefer to steer my boat into the din of roaring breakers"' (338). She goes off to New Mexico alone, leaving Fred with the resolution to 'attack her when his lance was brighter' (363). Thea is not seduced by her lover; they meet on equal terms and she feels no moral or religious qualms. It is her dignity which is outraged, not her conscience, when she discovers that Fred is already married.

The fact that Cather provides Fred with a mad wife is seen by many critics as proof of her 'peculiarity'. The argument runs that Cather never married because she was wedded to her art and, as she thought art and matrimony incompatible, she rigged the plot. But the terms in which this argument is invariably couched betray, not only bias, but what one might call the 'biographical fallacy'. Woodress, for example, states that she 'had no need of heterosexual relationships; she was married to her art' and, he concludes, it is not 'surprising that in her fiction artists never have happy marriages'. Now, she either had no need of heterosexual relationships because she was homosexual, or had no need of any relationships because she was an artist. The fallacy operates by assuming that she was 'eccentric' or 'peculiar' (rather loaded euphemisms) and then finding corroboration of this in the novels. But it is not there. Although Randall 'deduces' from his reading, 'not only a deep fear of emotional entanglements on Willa Cather's part but also a belief that art could and should be used as a substitute for a continued physical relationship', this is not a deduction but an imposition.[18]

*The Song of the Lark* is a portrait of an artist, not a study of married life. In the epilogue the reader learns that Fred and Thea marry and are happy – but that has not been Cather's primary concern. The notion of the Catheran artist as celibate is further undermined by the novel's treatment of sensuality, for Cather attributes Thea's artistic maturity to her awakened sexuality. Thea's transformation occurs while she and Fred are at Panther Cañon in the American Southwest. The lovers clamber up cliff walks, sleep in caves and bathe in freshwater streams. They inhabit an elemental world, free from the artificial restraints of society. Full of physical exuberance and energy, it is one of the most open-air portrayals of passion in literature.

In Chicago, Thea had been grinding at music lessons, accompanying, and singing at funerals but here she is revitalised. Later, Fred finds justification for his 'crooked' behaviour in her metamorphosis. Harsanyi, Thea's first teacher in Chicago, maintained that musical training and talent are not everything: to become an artist one had to be born again. In his analysis, emotional and sexual maturity play an important part. Before she meets Fred, Harsanyi tells her that she has not yet come into her gift and the woman she was meant to be: '"When you find your way to that gift and that woman, you will be at peace"' (265). Her rebirth is effected to a very large extent by Fred who helps her to find herself at Panther Cañon. She becomes a true artist. Indeed, she is almost a Wagnerian heroine; emanating a mythic aura, 'a wealth of *Jugendzeit*' with the same radiance and power as Sieglinde and Brünnhilde.

Cather had long been attracted to Wagner's heroines. In an early review she had disparaged, with a sweeping generalisation, the women of Rossini, Donizetti and Verdi: 'When Wagner called his goddess women down out of Valhalla, they relegated the fragile heroines of the old Italian operas to the oblivion of antiquated dolls on the shelves of a toy shop.'[19] To Cather, one of Wagner's greatest innovations had been in making his women active, animating forces in the drama. This clearly engaged her sympathy and provided a stimulus to the creation of Thea's character. The night before she makes her début as Sieglinde, she exhibits the catalepsy of the true Wagnerian heroine: 'she slept ten hours without turning over' and awoke 'in shining armour' (565).

The love duet from Act I of *Die Walküre* provides Cather with the perfect, though unstated, analogue for Fred and Thea's relationship. Her description of it emphasises the physicality of Thea's performance so that the part and the person playing it become indistinguishable: 'Into one lovely attitude after another the music swept her, love impelled her'. Drawing on her own experience, Sieglinde's story becomes Thea's:

> And the voice gave out all that was best in it. Like the Spring indeed, it blossomed into memories and prophecies, it recounted and it foretold, and she sang the story of her friendless life, and of how the thing that was truly herself, 'bright as the day, rose to the surface' when in the hostile world she for the first time beheld her Friend. (568)

Sieglinde's discovery of a true or second self, her transformation through love, parallel the events at Panther Cañon. Indeed, the comparison is implicit in the novel as a whole: Thea, too, has been living in a hostile world; as Cather wrote in the preface, the book is largely concerned with her 'shifts to evade an idle, gaping world which is determined that no artist shall ever do his best.' She has to counter hostility in Moonstone, even in her family, and jealousy and resentment in the musical society of Chicago; in short, the whole panorama of 'Stupid Faces'.

In the attempt to convey the emotional effect of Wagner's scene, the passion of the music, Cather employs an explicit sexual image. The sword, with which Siegmund is to defeat Hunding, is made into a symbol of love: 'Laughing, singing, exulting – with their passion and their sword – the *Volsungs* ran out into the spring night' (569). Cather heightens Sieglinde's role; one almost imagines that it is she who tears *Nothung* from the tree and at one point she appears like a sword herself, 'tall and shining like a Victory' (568). The emphasis on the mutality of their passion recalls the scenes of Thea and Fred's affair. The phrasing, too, echoes earlier descriptions: when Thea kissed Fred she rose 'straight and free', he felt her 'flash' and 'expan[d]' (405). They too 'kept laughing' and 'were delighted with each other' (407). The scene is crucial to the novel because it demonstrates Cather's belief in the importance of love in the creation of an artist and refutes the ubiquitous accusation that she refused to allow her female characters to be 'truly lovers'.[20] Thea does not find her gift and 'the woman she was meant to be' until in the hostile world she first beholds her Friend.

The performance of *Die Walküre* occurs at the end of the book and is Thea's crowning achievement. The clamorous applause signals an illustrious career for the heroine. But the final image is of the spent prima donna making her lonely way home. Cather clearly intended to illicit the reader's sympathy but this has not always been forthcoming. It is a convention in literature (particularly evident in *Evelyn Innes*) for an actress or singer to rise to fame, not just on the merit of her talent but through charm, good looks and, invariably, male patronage. Thea, however, fights her own way with inflexible determination and male critics in particular have found this unprepossessing. The terms in which Randall, for example, discusses her character betray a masculine bias against the asssertive and successful woman: she is 'a rough and aggressive woman' with 'despicable qualities'; so 'irritatingly aggressive' and 'unattractive', indeed, she seems to offer a personal insult to his ideas of femininity.[21]

In the creation of Thea's character it has been suggested that Cather drew on her own experience (for the early sections) and that of her friend, the Wagnerian soprano, Olive Fremstad.[22] This, I am sure, is right but the influence of Wagner's *Mein Leben* is also apparent. To Cather, as to many, Wagner was the archetypal artist not for his music alone but because he was a man of action who, despite indifference and hostility, coerced the society in which he lived to take art seriously. Thea fights the same battle. From the philistine to the dilettante, she exclaims, '"Nobody on God's earth wants it, *really*!"' (557). The qualities Cather revered in Wagner she gave to Thea. Elizabeth Sergeant recalls how Cather admired *Mein Leben*: 'he didn't stop to plead his own cause, or pause to meditate – just recorded action'. Cather never justifies Thea's actions. Fred tells her, '"You've no time to sit round and analyse your conduct or your feelings."'[23]

Another aspect of Thea's characterisation, the emphasis on personality, has often been misunderstood. In analysing Thea's particular genius, for example, Landry says: '"It's personality; that's as near as you can come to it."' By this he does not mean mere self-expression. Reading on, one discovers Landry attempting a closer definition: '"It's unconscious memory, maybe, inherited memory, like folk music. I call it personality."'[24] Thea's distinctive and original interpretations of the great Wagnerian roles are informed by indigenous folk memory; a process which parallels Cather's novelistic strategy of adapting European forms to accommodate American experience. The process itself seems to originate in the importance Wagner assigned to the retrospective vision and the reinterpretation of experience. Reminiscing with Dr Archie, Thea remarks, '"Wagner says . . . art is only a way of remembering youth"'.[25] Thea is sustained by the past and memories surface at each stage of her development; she also draws on the 'unconscious' or 'inherited' memory of the 'longer' past she discovers at Panther Cañon. Thus Cather employs two central features of Wagnerism: the recapture of the past by leitmotif, and the exploitation of national myth.

One example of Cather's use of motivic recall is a musical allusion which is introduced at the beginning of the novel and which is last heard in Part V. Thea's childhood piano teacher is a German named Wunsch; a

man of genuine musical ability whom sadness and exile
have driven to alcoholism. When he is forced to leave
Moonstone (after a drinking bout) he presents Thea with
an old score of Gluck's *Orfeo ed Euridice,* inscribed, 'Einst,
O Wunder' (120). The primary significance of the Orpheus
legend, here, is not that of the musician imposing order on
the natural world but the condition imposed upon him, not
to look back. Wunsch, the only major character who does
not reappear to share in Thea's success, departs for even
bleaker regions than Moonstone. When Thea leaves home
she knows that the parting is final but, like Orpheus, she
cannot turn back. The *Orfeo* score acts as her passport
to the Kingdom of Art. After completing her studies in
Chicago, she sails for Europe and is forced this time to
turn her back on Fred. Once again she packs 'the clumsily
bound' score which she takes with her into each new phase
of her life. Unlike Orpheus, Thea never weakens, but the
myth heightens the reader's awareness of her renunciation.

The aria which Wunsch teaches Thea is, 'Ach, ich
habe sie verloren'. Wunsch arrived in Moonstone with
nothing but the vestiges of musical talent and his memories.
Thea walks home in the snow after the class, leaving
him at the piano:

> Wunsch always came back to the same thing:
> 'Ach, ich habe sie verloren,
> . . .
> Euridice, Euridice!' (92–93)

As Fritz Kohler and his wife, the old German couple
with whom he lives, listen to him play, they recall their
homeland: 'From time to time Fritz sighed softly. He,
too, had lost a Euridice.' On the eve of her embarka-
tion for Europe, terrified at the possibility of failure,
Thea recalls Wunsch: 'she could still hear the old man
playing in the snowstorm. "Ach, ich habe sie verloren"'

(466). It is the motif of the exiles; those who have lost their country, their love or their art.

Having been disappointed so often by youthful talent, Wunsch had hardly dared to hope that Thea might develop into an artist. His inscription, 'Einst, O Wunder', reflects his longing that the failure of his own life might be redeemed by Thea. It comes from Beethoven's 'Adelaide': 'One day, O miracle, upon my grave shall bloom/A flower from the ashes of my heart'. His last view of Thea is a beautiful evocation of these lines:

> Yes, she was like a flower full of sun, but not the soft German flowers of his childhood . . . she was like the yellow prickly-pear blossoms that open there in the desert; thornier and sturdier than the maiden flowers he remembered; not so sweet, but wonderful (122).

Subtly, Cather fuses the Old World with the New: the flower of Beethoven's song is transformed into the American prickly-pear as Thea becomes the 'wonder' who rises from the ashes of Wunsch's ruined life.

The Gluck/Beethoven combination is one of several motifs used by Cather to structure the novel. (Some recurrences are restricted to the function of what Debussy termed 'calling cards': Spanish Johnny enters to the sound of Mexican ballads, Dr Archie is associated with Scottish airs and Thea's other childhood friend, the brakeman Ray Kennedy, with railway ditties.) Although there is not space to deal with them all here, these motifs of recollection act as linking devices, joining past to present and creating a web of connections between characters. The same kind of associations are made between Thea's present and the ancient past discovered at Panther Cañon through which she comes into contact with the mythic origins of America.

Cather's understanding of the operation of myth parallels Wagner's. Having abandoned the imitative modes of his earliest operas, he discovered the mainspring of his new art works in the resuscitation of Nordic mythology, and Cather, having abandoned the Jamesian mode of *Alexander's Bridge*, found hers in the excavation of Indian history. The value of myth to both artists is well illuminated by Nietzsche:

> Without myth, however, every culture loses its healthy creative natural power . . . The mythical figures have to be the invisibly omnipresent genii, under the care of which the young soul grows to maturity, by the signs of which the man gives a meaning to his life and struggles.[26]

The invisible genii in *A Song of the Lark* are the Navaho women. Walking on the paths their feet had worn smooth, examining their beautifully decorated water jars, Thea 'began to have intuitions about the women' (376) and gains a new meaning in her life.

In Nietzschean terms America would be 'doomed to exhaust all its possibilities' because it had no roots from which to feed its culture. Cather dramatises the dilemma of the 'mythless condition' – 'eternally hungering' for knowledge – through Thea: 'Her mind was like a rag bag into which she had been frantically thrusting whatever she could grab' (380). She makes the same discovery, of a 'primitive seat', that Nietzsche ascribed to Wagner: 'beneath this restlessly palpitating civilised life and educational convulsion there is concealed a glorious, intrinsically healthy, primeval power.' She is filled with 'vitality'; a lightness in the body and a driving power in the blood' (381). She throws away 'the lumber' she had acquired in Chicago: 'Her ideas were simplified, became sharper and clearer. She felt united and strong' (380).

Thea's apprehension of a mythic past and its relation to her as an artist is effected by the pottery jars of the Indian women. The 'beautiful decoration' reveals to her the origin of art: 'They had not only expressed their desire, but they had expressed it as beautifully as they could. Food, fire, water and something else . . . the seed of sorrow, and of so much delight' (379). The moment in which she makes this connection needs to be quoted in some length.

> When Thea took her bath at the bottom of the cañon, in the sunny pool behind the screen of cottonwoods, she sometimes felt as if the water must have sovereign qualities, from having been the object of so much service and desire. That stream was the only living thing left of the drama that had been played out in the cañon centuries ago. In the rapid, restless heart of it, flowing swifter than the rest, there was a continuity of life that reached back into the old time. The glittering thread of current had a kind of lightly worn, loosely knit personality, graceful and laughing . . .
>
> One morning . . . something flashed through her mind that made her draw herself up and stand still . . . The stream and the broken pottery: what was any art but an effort to make a sheath, a mould in which to imprison for a moment the shining elusive element which is life itself – life hurrying past us and running away, too strong to stop, too sweet to lose? The Indian women had held it in their jars. In the sculpture she had seen in the Art Institute, it had been caught in a flash of arrested motion. (378)

The central image of running water is concerned with life as ceaseless change and motion which can only be 'arrested' by art. As the ancient women made jars, Thea must make a vessel of her throat to capture the beauty of evanescence. Art is the only source of permanent value. The stream shows her the continuity of life, 'reaching back into the past', and her desire to sheathe it for a moment binds her to 'a long chain of human endeavour' (380).

Cather creates a legendary environment in which Thea's recognition can take place: the bath has 'a ceremonial gravity'; 'the atmosphere of the cañon was ritualistic' (378). In this context the 'drama that had been played out in the cañon centuries ago' has resonances of another drama, played in the deep gorges of the banks of the Rhine, in *Das Rheingold*. Thea bathes in her pool like the Rhinemaidens circling the bed of the river. Their laughter and gaiety and constant movement is reflected in the description of the water as 'rapid and restless', 'graceful and laughing'. The bright gleam of the Rhinegold, which shines and flashes as it breaks through the water, is like the 'glittering thread of current' in Thea's stream which, she feels, has 'sovereign qualities'. The shining and elusive element of the Rhinegold becomes life itself which must be captured, not like Alberich for the exercise of power, but for the creation of art.

Although Thea is an interpretative artist her epiphany is related to the process of creation. Her realisation that 'art was but an attempt . . . to imprison for a moment the shining, elusive element which is life itself' could hardly be closer to Cather's prescription for the novel: 'out of the teeming, gleaming stream of the present it must select the eternal material of art.[27] Thea's growth as an artist is a mirror of Cather's development and the insights Thea gains at the canon are very much Cather's own: the importance of myth and memory, of art as simplification, of allowing material to find its natural and inevitable form; above all in the connection between European art forms and American experience.

In 1932 Cather revised *The Song of the Lark*. She reduced the original version by about one-tenth and most of the cuts occur in the final section. For the most part the deleted passages are discussions of art and artists and many further allusions to Wagner. One might attribute the novel's unprecedented length in her canon, to the influence of Wagner's grand scale and perhaps it is not most of the cuts occur in the final section. For the most part the deleted passages are discussions of art and artists and many further allusions to Wagner. One might attribute the novel's unprecedented length in her canon, to the influence of Wagner's grand scale and perhaps it is not mere coincidence that the most overtly Wagnerian of all her novels should be the most ponderous. In a letter to Dorothy Canfield in 1930, Cather wrote that she had once tried to tell everything about a young person (in *The Song of the Lark*) and that she thought it a mistake. As one cannot tell everything she had come to think one must tell very little.

*One of Ours* (1922) marks another stage in Cather's involvement with Wagner; more sophisticated and less direct. Indeed at first sight it does not appear to have anything to do with music drama: a Western story without a frontier, it is concerned with one intelligent but untalented boy's inability to give his life any meaning until he discovers art, civilisation and finally death, in France. The critical outcry with which it was received centred largely on the novel's final section, 'Bidding the Eagles of the West Fly On'. Some, like Hemingway, objected to a woman writing a war novel at all, while others were dismayed by what they considered to be Cather's flag-waving cele-bration of 'our boys' in France.[28] A careful reading, of course, precludes any such interpretation. Further, her letters reveal that she was not primarily interested in the war but in the life of the protaganist.

In a series of letters to Dorothy Canfield, Cather gives an unusually full account of the novel's genesis. She protests that she never wanted to write a war story and that the book was in fact based on the life of her cousin, Grosvenor. She says that they were very much alike and very different; that he could never escape from the misery of being himself except in action and that whatever he put his hand to turned out either ugly or ridiculous. When he was killed at Cantigny in 1918 she was moved that anything people's inability to read the book as an imaginative work. She wrote to Elizabeth Moorhead of how disconcerting it was to have Claude regarded as a sentimental glorification of war, when he was clearly a farm boy; neither very old nor very wise. She explains how she tried to treat the war without any attempt at literalness, but as if it had been some war way back in history, as she was only interested in its impact on one boy. She denies that it was ever intended as a representation of the American soldier and regrets that she had not persevered with the original title, *Claude*.[29]

*Claude* may not have been an inspired appellation but *One of Ours* is disastrous; inviting precisely the reading she was so dismayed to receive. The final choice indicates in fact how perilously close she was to glorifying the war. Although Cather found it disconcerting, she was not unprepared for the critical onslaught. Indeed, she had never tried to pre-empt the possibility by sending an advance copy to H. L. Mencken with a letter pleading his indulgence and another, almost identical, to Carl Van Doren.[30] So far as I am aware this was an unprecedented move and one which she never repeated. In the letter to Mencken she begins humbly by conceding that *One of Ours* is very different from her previous novels and may be a mistake. If he thinks she has done a sickly, sentimental, old-maid job, she exhorts him to tell her so loudly, like a man, to rub it in and pound it down. Mencken duly obliged and accused her of writing like *The Ladies' Home Journal*. The sparring tone of her letter to him reflects her uneasiness at having ventured into the exclusively male preserve of war. But despite her bravado, she confessed to Dorothy Canfield that the final section was not so successful as the earlier parts, which dealt with Claude's life on the farm. She rewrote it several times but was still unhappy with the style.

In the letter to Mencken she laments that presentation is always a gamble and that the road is so rutted with old tracks, we cannot go on as we would. One of the paths she had explored was Wagner's *Parsifal*. It appears that 'Bidding the Eagles of the West Fly On' was at one stage entitled, 'The Blameless Fool by Pity Enlightened'. In a letter to a Mr Johns she congratulates him on being the first sleuth to dig the Parsifal theme out of Claude Wheeler – which she thought she had buried so deep! She relates how all through the first part of the book she had kept promising herself that she would put Wagner's subtitle where she eventually put a line from Vachel Lindsay. She concludes that either he or she did pretty well, when the theme got through to him out of absolute and consistent reticence. Unfortunately, she is equally reticent about why she changed her mind. Perhaps she felt that in its final form the comparison between Claude and Parsifal was too tenuous, or as she phrased it, too deep. Clearly she felt no compunction about drawing on a German model but she may have deemed it impolitic to advertise the fact that she had done so, especially as by the time Wagner wrote *Parsifal* he had become quite chauvinistic. A letter to Elizabeth Moorhead suggests that this may have influenced her decision: she complains that if a story happens to touch upon people's political opinions they cannot see it as an imaginative thing at all – it is as if a pianist in the middle of a sonata began to play 'The Watch on the Rhine' in wartime.[31] This passage occurs in an account of the abusive letters she had received from pacifists. Ironically, if she had put 'The Simple Fool by Pity Enlightened' it might have appeased those readers who assumed, on the contrary, that she was pounding out 'The Yanks are Coming'.

The question remains as to why, in a story of an American farm boy, she should have looked to Wagner at all. Possibly, this was to put a distance between herself and the character of Claude and, as she was so nervous about the war episodes, she may have hoped that the Wagnerian parallel would provide a supporting structure. Hemingway scornfully accused her of Catherising *A Birth of a Nation* but far from seeking a realistic model, she was anxious to avoid the specific connotations of The Great War. By infusing a legendary element she wanted to escape the political opinions and prejudices which would otherwise distract from her real theme. The attempt was a failure and it was perhaps naive of her to imagine that Claude's story could be disengaged from its social and political context. However, if the *Parsifal* analogy had been more in evidence, then the events in France might have been seen as belonging uniquely to Claude's personal salvation, as she had intended. Just as Parsifal is initiated into the mysteries of the Holy Grail, Claude is introduced to the Kingdom of Art (France): both are enlightened through pity and become agents of redemption; Parsifal defeats Klingsor and Claude the mysterious German officer.

Cather's letters during this period reflect her preoccupation with Wagner. She tells Dorothy Canfield how she was compelled to write the book because of her blood identity with Grosvenor and the bond between them like Siegmund and Sieglinde – the woes of the Volsungs. But they also reveal that she was juggling with two very different aims and procedures. First, she was concerned to restrict the authorial voice to the scope of a first-person narration so that the reader apprehends Calude's experience through his eyes and with his understanding. Cather uses a kind of reported speech, employing only language appropriate to him: for example, 'When Claude joined his company at the station, they had the laugh on him' (343). She told Canfield that she had tried to make a narrative that is always Claude and not her writing about France or doughboys. However, while Claude provides the novel's point of view, Cather wanted at the same time to frame this within the *Parsifal* analogy.

In one sense the work suited her purpose exactly: both Parsifal and Claude are ignorant simpletons, wanderers seeking adventure, aimless and without identity; the Grail brotherhood's holy war finds its counterpart in the American army's fight, as it was believed, to save freedom and democracy; and Parsifal's initiation into the mystery of the Grail is like Claude's induction to the mysteries of music and art. The latter point of comparison is particularly highlighted. David Gerhardt, Claude's fellow officer, takes him to the Fleury household, where 'Music ha[d] always been like a religion' (418), and which might be seen as a kind of Grail Castle. Lucien, the younger son of the family, fetches the Amati and presents it as if he were performing a holy rite: 'He opened [the case] carefully and took off the velvet cloth as if this was his particular office.' The violin has the same function as the Grail. The association of the two is highlighted by Gerhardt's account of how his Stradivarius had been smashed to pieces in a car wreck and the destruction had presaged the war which was to ensue. Since that time he has found it almost too painful to play. In *Parsifal* the wounded Amfortas refuses to perform the Grail rites and so the survival of the brotherhood is threatened.

In *One of Ours* the holy flame of the Grail is rekindled for a moment as Gerhardt plays and Claude watches Lucien: 'in each of his black eyes a candle flame was reflected, as if some steady fire were actually burning there' (416). The episode at the Fleury house is one of the decisive moments in Claude's growth of awareness, just as Parsifal's attendance at the Grail ceremony is in his. Their respective experiences are only partial revelations: Parsifal is moved but uncomprehending while Claude, who had never had the opportunity to study or travel, remains locked in a bitter and resentful sense of his own ignorance.

The ability to incorporate a mythic element into a narration of ordinary events, which Cather attempted in earlier stories, comes to full maturity here. However, despite the success with which the Grail motif is introduced, Cather's two aims are almost mutually exclusive, for a narrative that is always Claude cannot at the same time be *Parsifal*, particularly as Wagnerian music drama could not be more remote from Claude's cultural awareness. It is from this contradiction, perhaps, that much of her uneasiness stemmed and which explains why the *Parsifal* theme was buried so deep.

None the less, some of the bones of the skeleton still show. For example, at Beaufort – the counterpart to Klingsor's magic garden. As the men are all in the army, only the flower maidens remain: 'The sun was shining, for a change, – everything was looking cheerful. The village seemed to be swarming with girls; some of them were pretty, and all were friendly' (428). Suddenly a shot rings out, for although the occupying force had decamped, a few German soldiers had been left behind. The shot comes from an officer hidden in the top-floor room of one of the houses. Claude rushes up and kills him with his bayonet, just as Parsifal defeats Klingsor with a spear.

The officer is an extremely mysterious figure: hanging round his neck 'was a miniature case, and in it was a painting, – not, as Bert romantically hoped when he opened it, of a beautiful woman, but of a young man, pale as snow, with blurred forget-me-not eyes' (431). Although the incident is taken from one of the many war experiences related to Cather by wounded soldiers whom she visited in hospital in New York, it is cleverly worked into the *Parsifal* framework. The decadent German officer becomes Klingsor. The magician's downfall is a victory for the Grail brotherhood and the officer's death signals the defeat of the German army.

Despite the general influence, it would be impossible to impose a Wagnerian scheme on the sequence of scenes which make up the novel's final section. The parallel cannot be said to extend very far which has no Kundry, no Amfortas, and only a rather implausible Gurnemanz in the character of Gerhardt. Nor can one isolate the revelatory moment of pity that Parsifal experiences through Kundry's kiss. Further, although *Parsifal* provided a means of

conveying a legendary atmosphere, its triumphant denoue-
ment is wholly inappropriate. Unlike Parsifal, Claude dies
and there is no restitution of divine order, only a very
ambiguous victory for good intentions. The breathtaking
beauty of the 'Miracle of Supreme Salvation' has no
place in *One of Ours* which ends with Mrs Wheeler's
(Herzeleide?) poignant realisation that her son's belief
in a 'glorious' 'cause' (458) was a delusion.

Any imputation of fatuous or belligerent patriotism is
surely negated by the novel's verdict that Claude 'died
believing his own country better than it is, and France better
than any country can ever be.' The one unequivocal belief
granted to him is in the value of art. As a codicil one might
add that Wagner named *Parsifal* a 'Buhnenweihfestspiel'
('Sacred stage festival play'), on the premise that since
art had become religion, religion could become art. Both
Wagner and Cather provoked a similar critical disgust: he
was accused of writing a sickly parody of the Mass and she
a sentimental glorification of war. What, on the contrary,
both works manifest is their creators' belief, as Cather said
in *The Professor's House*, that '"Art and religion (they
are the same thing, in the end, of course) have given
man the only happiness he has ever had"' (69).

Wagner and the redemptive power of art is also the theme
of 'Uncle Valentine' (1925).[32] The eponymous character is
an American song composer, who dies in a car accident
when he is barely thirty, and the story is narrated by a
woman who had known him in her youth, when they
were neighbours in the rural outskirts of Pittsburgh.
Marjorie, the narrator, and her sister, come to live with
their cousins and their Aunt Charlotte and Uncle Harry
at Fox Hill. The bulk of the story, divided into thirteen
sections or scenes, is concerned with Valentine Ramsay's
return to his family home, Bonnie Brae, where he spends
a year rambling in the hills with Charlotte and the little
girls, composing songs for them to sing. The idyll is

shattered when his ex-wife buys one of the neighbouring estates and takes possession of the countryside.

This long short story is an American *Götterdämmerung*. Bonnie Brae, built on a hill top – a household of lonely men once wealthy but now declined into neurosis, alcoholism and redundancy – is Valhalla. Pittsburgh, with its steel mills belching smoke is Nibelheim; its inhabitants, typified by Valentine's ex-wife, Janet Oglethorpe, are concerned only with the accumulation of wealth. The forges of Alberich's underworld kingdom are paralleled by Pittsburgh's heavy industry and by the end of the story, Bonnie Brae and Fox Hill have been pulled down to make way for the factories and mills. The life of the easy-going 'old' families is gone for good.

The central Wagnerian image occurs during one of Valentine's walks in the countryside with Charlotte and the Rhinemaidens:

> Suddenly, in the low cut between the hills across the river, we saw a luminousness, throbbing and phosphorescent, a ghostly brightness with mists streaming about it and enfolding it, struggling to quench it. We knew it was the moon, but we could see no form, no solid image; it was a flowing, surging, liquid gleaming; now stronger, now softer.

> 'The Rhinegold!' murmured Valentine and Aunt Charlotte in one breath.

Valentine never imagines that the land belongs to anyone but when the Oglethorpes buy it the place loses its innocence, just as the Rhinegold becomes corrupt once Alberich gets hold of it. The Ramsays, living on the remains of ancestral wealth and producing nothing themselves, cannot outbid the Oglethorpes who have solid, industrial money behind them. In the same way, Wotan and the gods decline into weakness and cannot pay for Valhalla.

When they return from their walk to Charlotte's house, Valentine plays excerpts from the *Ring* cycle on the piano. Recalling the days when Walter Damrosch produced Wagner's operas in America, he asks, '"Why can't people stay young forever?"' Wagner's gods are kept alive by Freia but at Bonnie Brae there is no goddess of eternal youth, only the rather sinister housekeeper, Molla Carsen, who exercises a mysterious control over her employers. The crumbling of the Ramsays' way of life is inevitable; they belong to a vanishing order which they are powerless to uphold. Although Cather clearly dislikes the new era, the story is not indulgently nostalgic; with the exception of Valentine, the Ramsays are weak, shabby, useless. In the *Ring*, Wotan begets Siegmund and Sieglinde in the hope that they will produce the hero, Siegfried, to save Valhalla but Valentine, the only one in his family with a child, sees himself as the end of the line: '"My son Dickie, he'll be an Oglethorpe! He'll get on and won't carry this damned business any further."'

'Uncle Valentine' is not only about the decline of the 'old' American families and the rise of industrialism, it is also an exploration of the creative process; how it is fostered and how crushed. Valentine composes his best songs at Bonnie Brae: 'the place was vocal to him.' In the prologue, a young singer asks what prevented Ramsay from composing. Louise Ireland, once his lover in Paris, replies: '"The things that always prevent one: marriage, money, friends, the general social order."' These had not prevented Wagner, of course, who abandoned his first wife, took whatever money he could get his hands on, abused his friends and bent the social order to accommodate his will. Valentine is very much influenced by the Master; he rushes to Bayreuth to escape his wife and composes a song cycle based on the legend of Tristan and Iseult, but he has neither Wagner's monomania nor his stature as an artist. Valentine produces about thirty songs, Wagner a dozen or more operas.

By the time Cather came to write 'Uncle Valentine' her admiration for Wagner's personality seems to have softened. She had once relished the spectacle of Wagner trampling on everyone and extolled him as the archetypal artist. One can see a little of this fervour permeating her conception of Thea; indeed, *The Song of the Lark* is infused with the ethos of success and of the end justifying the means. Cather was enamoured by the prospect of someone 'fighting her way', battling against society, but in time she grew more concerned with the creative faculty itself; its imperfections, its fragility and the fugitive nature of the artist's gift. She became less exigent in her demands; an unassuming man composing a few beautiful songs was then something to be treasured. 'Uncle Valentine' is a mature and sensitive presentation of the artist, a gentle and moving account of defeat, one of her finest stories, to be read '*adagio non troppo*'.

This marks the end of Cather's excursions into music drama: she raided Wagner's work for twenty-five years, bringing back plots, ideas and imagery and she found, both in the man and his music, a powerful artistic catalyst. She was unique amongst Americans to explore the territory that had been opened up by him. In 1935 she returned once more to the subject of the artist's life, in *Lucy Gayheart,* but the young pianist's trials and death by drowning are portrayed without Wagnerian reverberations. On the contrary, as Richard Giannone shows, the story is greatly indebted to *Die Winterreise*.[33] But though it sometimes catches Schubert's poignancy, it never achieves his profundity or grace. Interestingly, Edith Lewis relates how Cather went to the opera far less in the 1930s and 40s and that she listened more often to chamber music; abandoning Wagner for Beethoven's late quartets.[34] The element of grandiloquence, perhaps, had begun to pall and her own work had long since taken a new direction. She had tried 'the full-blooded' method in *The Song of the Lark* and found it did not wholly suit her. There were still aspects of Wagner's genius which she admired and his music remained for her a constant source of affirmation and an enduring testimony to the value of art. As Charlotte Waterford says, '"What a difference Wagner made in the world, after all."'

In a speech given to the 'Friends of the Princeton University Library' in 1933, it is evident that Cather still associated Wagner with the craft of fiction and its future:

> The novel, if it can be called a form of art, is a new arrival among the arts and its most interesting developments are still to come. All the other arts are centuries older. Looking back over its short history, perhaps the most interesting thing one notices about the novel is its amazing elasticity and variety. Like the Tarnhelm which the Nibelungs made for Alberich, this lightly woven net of words has the power of transformation, can present a giant, a dragon, a mouse or a worm.[35]

Her own oeuvre alone is a testament to the novel's protean possibilities, with each work an attempt 'to arrest the stream of life' and to transform the lives of men and women into art.

# 3 From horse opera to homesteads:
## O Pioneers!

> Lift up a song,
> My sweaty men,
> Lift up a song.
> Sherwood Anderson, 'Song of the Sap'[1]

Cather saw herself as a literary sod-buster, breaking new ground despite indifference and even hostility. She put Nebraska on the map at a time when America's literary establishment was determined not to recognise its existence. On the publication of *O Pioneers!* (1913) one New York critic said, 'I simply don't give a damn what happens in Nebraska, no matter who writes about it.' Perhaps nobody ever would, had it not been for Cather. Whereas Hardy's Wessex, say, with its distinctive geography, history, native inhabitants and customs, seemed intrinsically worth being written about, Nebraska was featureless, raw, populated only by immigrants and drifters; part of the vast, undifferentiated Midwest. As Cather ruefully remarked, it was 'distinctly déclassé as a literary background.'[2]

Out of this recalcitrant material she created a country, as distinctive as Hardy's and with the same universal appeal. Through *O Pioneers!*, *The Song of the Lark*, *My Ántonia*, *One of Ours*, *Obscure Destinies* and *Lucy Gayheart* one can trace the landmarks of Cather country; the Divide, the prairies and creeks, the Republican Valley, the small frontier town which, whether it is called Black Hawk, Hanover or Moonstone is always Red Cloud – and become familiar with the inhabitants; characters who are not only uniquely her own but inseparable from the country she created, much as Tess Durbeyfield could only belong to Hardy and his Wessex. In Cather's fictional territory the land was given a cultural identity; a unique achievement in the literature of the American Midwest.

None the less, literary criticism until recently has insisted on categorising Cather as an old-fashioned local colourist. Held to be regional and agrarian and therefore peripheral to modern, urban America, she became increasingly neglected in the years following her death. The appellation 'local colourist' is the kiss of death for an American writer, suggesting either the polite works of lady authors or the mildly humorous dialect stories of the 'father' of Western local colour, Bret Harte. Moreover, 'sectionalism', as it is also called, is invariably subsumed under the two broad divisions of Eastern and Western literature, which are inevitably seen in opposition to each other, with the latter being decidedly the poor relation. To be classified as a Western local colourist guarantees one a place on the bottom rung of the literary ladder. Acutely aware of this in her youth, Cather attempted to become Eastern; busied herself with the romance of drawing rooms and literary salons and made a series of false starts. When she began to write in her own voice it was not, as was the case with so many of her compatriots, by spurning the East and becoming aggressively Western but by transcending the opposition between the two.

Cather's early stories – including those she did not collect for republication – may be divided into two main categories: those set in the Midwest, and those dealing with artists and Eastern society; some are about the frustrations of being an artist in the Midwest and appeared in her first published volume, *The Troll Garden* (1905). Her first novel, the Jamesian *Alexander's Bridge*, was published in 1912,

a year before *O Pioneers!*, which is generally held to
be the first of her mature works, written in her own
style and dealing with what has come to be regarded
as authentic Cather material. However, it seems to me,
that this assessment of *O Pioneers!* is only partially true,
or rather, true in parts: at the time of writing, Cather was
still very nervous about writing of the West and anxious to
gain the approval of the literary establishment in the East.

The seemingly interminable interest in the polarisation
of the East and West of America has afflicted not only
critics and historians but American writers too. For many
years Cather herself was drawn into the East/West debate
and vacillated between the two; loathing the philistine West
and looking to the East as the seat of civilisation, from there
looking back to the West with nostalgia and regret. But at
this point it might be helpful to place Cather in the historical
context of the East/West debate in order to show its effect on
her and how she escaped this crippling duality.

The issue is the legacy of colonial times. The attempt to
create an authentic, indigenous American literature, distinct
particularly from the English, began to dominate in the early
nineteenth century. Emerson, though not perhaps the first,
was one of the most influential figures in this movement.
In his essay 'The American Scholar' (1837) he complained,
'we have listened too long to the courtly Muses of Europe',
and his call to 'speak our own minds' was echoed with
increasing vociferation.[3] It was not just post-colonial resentment but a feeling that the New World needed new forms to
accommodate and express a new experience of life. During
the latter half of the nineteenth century the Western writers
joined in and complained not only of England but of the East
(still to some extent England's representative) which had
become the dominant literary centre in America. Western
writers betrayed a similar mixture of resentment and envy,
coupled with a sense of the uniqueness of the Western
American experience which had yet to be portrayed.

Hamlin Garland's *Crumbling Idols* (1837), for example, is an extended diatribe against England, the East of America and the West's eagerness to conform to their standards.[4] This dependence, he argued, meant that the Middle States had no literature of their own except 'dime novels'. Writers had been blind to the 'special picturesqueness of the West' which had been ignored by the East and denigrated by the West itself. The field was wide open for the Western writer who had the courage to stay at home. At the time Garland published *Crumbling Idols*, Cather was twenty-one and already writing but she was not ready to accept his challenge. Nebraska seemed barren, Lincoln a backwater and she longed, to use Garland's phrase, 'to discuss dead issues in English literature' in Boston.

The Midwest was too wide open; there was nothing for a young writer to sieze hold of, only an empty horizon and a geological past. Both the literal and the literary landscapes were without form. The Far West had a glamour of its own and could claim Mark Twain (1835–1910), Jack London (1876–1916) and, to some extent, Frank Norris (1870–1902). But the Middle States could boast of little better than Edward Eggleston's *The Hoosier Schoolmaster* (1871) or Edgar W. Howe's *The Story of a Country Town* (1883), neither of which displays to any remarkable degree 'the special picturesqueness of the West'. Nor for that matter do Garland's own books. For the most part they are chronicles of poverty, monotony and deprivation, written largely in reaction to the Easterner's idea of the West as a land of opportunity for rugged individualists. A story such as 'The Lion's Paw', for example, in *Main Travelled Roads* (1891) has as its sole purpose the exposure of an economic system in which struggling farmers, powerless to pay off exorbitant mortgage rates, went to the wall.

In all of this there was nothing to attract Cather who found Garland's writing utterly contemptible:

> No man ever tried his hand at fiction and persisted
> in the vain attempt who so utterly lacked these essen-
> tial things [imagination and style] as Mr. Garland.
> Art is temperament and Hamlin Garland has no more
> temperament than a prairie dog.

So far as she was concerned, Garland was not an artist but a journalist – and a depressing one – offering
only 'stern, ugly lessons in political economy'. Cather
made these comments in her early twenties when she
was very impressed by Henry James and not at all by
Nebraska. While she was working for the Lincoln *Journal*,
for example, she affected polite surprise on learning that a
play called *Nebraska* had actually been written:

> Just what there is in this particular part of the universe
> to make a play of it is difficult to say. Probably the drama
> will deal with, 'barren, windswept prairies, fields of
> stunted corn, whose parched leaves rattle like skeletons
> in the burning south wind', and all that sort of rot which
> Mr. Hamlin Garland and his school have seen fit to write
> about our peaceable and inoffensive country.[5]

She does not mention, of course, that she herself was
at that very moment churning out pages on the scorched
prairie theme. Indeed, when 'A Wagner Matinee' was
published it was her turn to be denounced by the *Journal*
for casting a slur on the State.

Cather rejected Garland because he failed to capture
the picturesqueness of the West. In her youth she herself
could not see it had any. She had been blind to the West,
as she told H. L. Mencken in 1922, because she had been
preoccupied with making an entrance in good society, in the
company of Henry James.[6] Considering it to be peripheral
and feminine, Cather had been determined not to write
'local colour': 'It is the element of women, they seldom

write about anything else.'[7] Despite her fears, Cather's mature achievement was to be triumphantly local and female, to make the local not only national but universal, to transform characteristics which had always been considered marginal and make them transcendent.

With some trepidation she published *O Pioneers!*. The unresolved conflict between the East and the West is evident in the title, taken from Walt Whitman, and the dedication to Sarah Orne Jewett and her 'beautiful and delicate work'. Cather's need to be sanctioned by the literary establishment in the East is central to the novel's failure. In 'My First Novels' Cather claims the book was not only original in subject but that it departed radically from literary convention: '*O Pioneers!* was set in Nebraska, of all places . . . [It] was not only about Nebraska farmers, the farmers were Swedes! . . . Since I wrote *O Pioneers!* for myself, I ignored all the situations and accents that were then thought to be necessary.'[8] As she says, the 'novel of the soil' had not then come into fashion in America and it took some daring to write about a Midwestern farming community. Cather's letters before the novel's publication express a mixture of defiance and fear; a novel all about crops seemed the most hopeless proposition on earth but it was what she wanted to do.[9] With James and Wharton still ruling the drawing room, while the younger generation were attacking the sprawling new cities, Cather was on her own.

But perhaps the major reason for the novel's 'lonesomeness' was because the central characters are immigrants. Before Cather, Swedes, Bohemians, French and Germans had figured, if at all, as minor characters (often broadly humorous); they had never been at the centre of Western literature. There is an episode in Sherwood Anderson's *Tar: A Midwest Childhood* (1926) which epitomises the position of the European pioneer in Western literature at that time. The young narrator is out walking one Sunday when he comes across some farmers threshing in the fields and thinks to himself: 'They must be some foreigners, like Germans or something. They can't be very civilized.' Tar stares at the country boys in 'surprise' and he is even more startled when women bring baskets of food into the fields. They offer him some but he is shocked and refuses. Tar is not hostile, indeed he is curious, but the Germans in the fields on Sunday 'seemed strange'; 'it was funny though'.[10] The whole episode has a quizzical air; the immigrants are odd but fascinating aliens viewed from outside. They provide only an afternoon's spectacle in Tar's Midwest childhood and they live in a world which remains unknown to the narrator. Before Cather, the immigrant in Western literature had the status of a literary untouchable.

To us now, perhaps the most extraordinary thing is not that Cather wrote about the immigrant but that other Western writers did not. Immigration was one of the most important factors in the settling of the Midwest and yet it seems as if Cather were almost the only one to recognise and respond to this at the time. From the 1870s onward there had been a massive influx of Europeans, so much so that when Henry James visited America in 1904 he felt shocked, dispossessed by 'the alien', and he longed for 'the luxury of some such close and sweet and *whole* national consciousness as that of the Switzer and the Scot'.[11] The immigrants were not for the most part Russian counts and Italian princesses but artisans, tailors and musicians, who contributed their crafts to their adopted country. It is somewhat ironic that it should have been Cather, so often accused of being conservative and anti-democratic, who embraced with open arms Whitman's 'race of races'; who saw the importance of the immigrant to America's future and celebrated their contribution to its culture.

Modern American literature is often traced in a line of descent from Sherwood Anderson and Sinclair Lewis, with Cather invariably being regarded as somehow marginal to the whole enterprise:

Her art is not a big art. It does not respond to
the troubled sense of American might and magnitude
realized but undirected, and felt so strongly by such
men as Sinclair Lewis in the same decades. It is
national in significance, but not in scope. Her col-
leagues among the men 'sweated sore' over that job,
whereas her books rose free and far more creative
than critical. She is preservative, almost antiquarian,
content with much space in little room – feminine in
this, and in her passionate revelation of the values
which conserve the life of the emotions.[12]

This, fairly typical, assessment of Cather's national importance boils down to an assertion that she is little, feminine
and preservative whereas the USA is big, masculine and
chaotic and anyway to be truly American one must sweat
a lot. And yet there is nothing small and ladylike about
Cather's work and surely a concern with values and
emotions is hardly exclusively feminine.

The issue would not in itself be of paramount importance
except that the obsession, on both sides of the Atlantic, with
the special characteristics of American literature, has meant
that Cather's writing has been pushed to the sidelines. In
*The Literature of the Unites States*, for example, Cunliffe
remarks on the limitations of the dominant, masculine tradition and yet he still does not discuss Cather – as a possible
corrective – in the chapter on Western literature, nor in
'Fiction since World War I', but throws her in with Harriet
Beecher Stowe, Sarah Orne Jewett and Emily Dickinson
among others, under the heading of 'Minor Key':

. . . women writers have made a quite special contribution to American literature. At its best, as in
Willa Cather and Ellen Glasgow (1874–1945), with its
attachment to place, to heritage and to family ties, it

has provided (like the piano in the shanty) a necessary counter-mood to the grandiose, outdoor, masculine
tendencies of American prose.[13]

Cunliffe is one of the most perceptive and sympathetic
of Cather's critics but he does not go far enough here. Her
contribution was more profound than a little tinkling of the
ivories on the lone prairie; an image which is too readily
associated with the idea that the pioneers were men who
forged ahead into the wilderness while the women came
up behind carrying tablecloths; the kind of machismo,
indeed, which informs *The Virginian* (1902), where the
West is 'a great playground' until the advent of the
school ma'am when the cowpunchers feared, 'it would
not long be a country for men'.[14] One might be very
glad it would not, but Cather knew it never had been.
That the dominant tradition in modern American
literature is male will surprise no one. Anderson,
Lewis, Hemingway, Fitzgerald, Dos Passos, Steinbeck
and Faulkner are generally held to be the writers who
defined the character of their time. That they should,
for the most part, have been so aggressively masculine
can perhaps be attributed to the gradual emergence of
Western literature as a serious and influential phenomenon
during the first half of the century. Anderson, for example,
although his reputation has since waned, was both popular
and highly esteemed in the 1920s and *Winesburg Ohio* (1919)
is still regarded as an American classic. Dubbed 'the
father' of Hemingway and Faulkner, he was enormously
influential and the man-to-man poetry of much modern
American prose can perhaps be traced back to him.
An exaggerated concern with manliness has been a
distinguishing feature of Western literature since the dime
novels about Jesse James, Buffalo Bill and that 'half
hoss, half alligator', Davy Crockett. It was cherished
because it was considered to be craggy and distinctive;

far removed from the effete civilisation of the East Coast. It appears in a muted though persistent form in Sherwood Anderson. His *Tar: A Midwest Childhood*, for example, establishes its exclusively masculine point of view in the foreword: 'I, Sherwood Anderson, an American man, in my youth did so and so' (ix). In the first chapter he candidly asks the reader, 'How are you, being a man, going to understand women?' (5). And Western manliness is always opposed to European culture:

> When he grew to be a man Tar saw Europe and liked it, but all the time he was there he had an American hunger . . . for waste places, roominess, . . . waste spaces for boys to play in – A man, if he is any good, never gets over being a boy. (166)

We are back once again with the sweaty philistine (who never grows up) as the authentic American.

Since Anderson and Cather were exact contemporaries, both Southerners who were transplanted West during childhood and later wrote from their early memories of small towns and farms in the Middle States, it is surprising that they are never compared. This is particularly unfortuante as Cather's portrayal of the West – influenced by the immigrant and European culture – provides an interesting perspective on Anderson's insistence on the sanctity of the Western American man, preserving his authorial integrity by rejecting European literature (particularly English) and harping on, not only about his Americanness but his masculinity; indeed, apparently incapable of distinguishing between the two. The presence of Anderson the man, in both the autobiographies and the more purely fictional works, also belongs to the modern American tendency for the author to be more important than his books and is in direct contrast with Cather's discipline, learned from Flaubert, of keeping oneself invisible.

Cather was not impressed by the macho West or its legacy. The former was a great distortion, as she intimated in a letter to a Mr Boynton, who had given *O Pioneers!* a favourable review. In it she thanks him for acknowledging that the cowpuncher's experience of the West was not the only possible one and for seeing that one might give a more truthful account of life in a new country without resorting to a jovial brutality which cannot, in any case, be successfully affected by a woman.[15] As for the latter, she was dismayed at the direction of contemporary American fiction. In an undated letter which, however, does mention Steinbeck and Saroyan, she refers to the prevailing fashion for writing in words of one syllable. She continues by saying that it is rather alarming to see the magnificent reach of the language silent, except for one octave, on which little boys seem to be pounding the same keys over and over with one finger.[16]

Cather's novels reveal a different West and they offered an alternative direction for American literature. They spoke for the Middlewestern immigrant and the woman, who had hitherto been silent, and they spoke in the language of an old culture taking root in a new land. Her radical contribution was to show that one could be an authentically American writer without resorting to, what she termed, cub-reporter slang, or abandoning the full scale of a language made resonant, at least to her, by Chaucer, The King James Bible and Shakespeare; that one could learn from the Muse of Europe without becoming imitative and second rate. She also created an alternative to the male mythology of the West. She showed that the pioneers were men and women and that the vast fields of wheat and corn which stretch across Middle America were foreseen and planted by characters such as Alexandra, a Swedish immigrant and a woman: 'The history of every country begins in the heart of a man or a woman' (65).

Cather's 'history' of the West begins with *O Pioneers!*. In 'The Wild Land' she describes the Bergson family, their neighbours and their battle to survive on the windy Nebraska tableland. While life is still hard and the crops uncertain, Mr Bergson dies and 'entrust[s] the future of his family and the possibilities of his hard-won land' to his daughter. He would much rather have been able to appoint his sons, Lou and Oscar, but he 'had to accept the situation as it was' (24). The remainder of Part I is mainly concerned with Alexandra's struggle to make the farm a success despite opposition from her brothers and the land itself.

The structure is episodic: Alexandra's visit to Hanover, Bergson's death, the trip to Crazy Ivar's, Carl Linstrum's departure after three years of drought and failed crops and finally Alexandra and Emil's survey of the more prosperous farms in the Republican Valley. It is not the plot-dominated novel of hero and heroine that characterises local colour. Indeed in a letter to Zoë Akins she wrote that the country is the hero – or the heroine – though she hoped the people were interesting too.[17] Her fear that crops and Swedes would bore everyone but herself is unfounded; the first part of the novel makes compelling reading. Without resorting to the sensationalism of her earliest stories, Cather evokes the homesteaders' fear and insecurity inspired by the bleak and inhospitable land they had come to settle: 'The homesteads were few and far apart; here and there a windmill gaunt against the sky, a sod house crouching in a hollow. But the great fact was the land itself, which seemed to overwhelm the little beginnings of human society that struggled in its sombre wastes' (15). As Cather intended, the land has a character of its own: 'It was still a wild thing that had its ugly moods' (20). As the novel progresses its character develops and so does Alexandra's relation to it.

After three years of drought and failed crops Alexandra's brothers want to sell the farm and move to the more fertile valley. Many of their neighbours are discouraged and leave while the 'smart men' in the town buy the land very cheaply. With the pioneer's uncanny blend of mysticism and materialism, Alexandra persuades her brothers to mortgage the farm and buy more of the apparently useless high land. Lou and Oscar are unwilling but she insists: '"Down there they have a little certainty, but up with us there is a big chance"' (64). She unites the 'Old World belief in land' with New World opportunism; the pioneer's big chance being the acceptable face of the American dream.

Part I ends with Alexandra's discovery of her love for the land and the first intimations of success: 'Under the long shaggy ridges, she felt the future stirring' (71). Part II opens sixteen years later with the struggle over. Alexandra is one of the biggest farmers in the region and the prairie has transformed itself into the land of milk and honey. Cather's leap into success represents a failure of nerve because she does not work towards it. It is as if she thought that seventy pages of crops and pigs was about as much as most readers could stand. Yet the novel's first part makes one regret that she did not have the courage to carry on. Instead, the book's final four-fifths are not only a falling off but a different kind of novel.

Alexandra, for example, is not a wholly convincing character in the later chapters. Originally she makes a very striking entrance, 'a tall, strong girl' walking 'rapidly and resolutely': 'she wore a man's long ulster (not as if it were an affliction, but as if it were very comfortable and belonged to her)' (6). She has a 'glance of Amazonian fierceness' and a dazzling head of 'reddish-yellow curls' (8). She is tender and protective towards her brothers, 'hard' only through necessity; a strong, independent, generous woman. In Part II there is a subtle difference; Alexandra becomes a corn goddess, statuesque and radiant. As she strides through the fields, showers her gleaming white body and presides over her household of farm hands and Swedish maids, she is an impressive combination of matriarch and myth. Lou remarks that '"Alexandra ain't much like other women folks"' (173) and cannot imagine her marrying.

Unfortunately, Cather gives her a lover and the result is ludicrous. After a sixteen-year absence, her childhood friend, Carl Linstrum, suddenly reappears. In Part I there isn't even the faintest whiff of romance but, during the first week of his return, they discuss marriage as if it had all been settled long ago that they were made for each other.

Cather was trying to burgle the house by throwing some red meat to the dogs. A love story between a corn goddess and her fields was too unconventional so she dragged back Carl, of the 'soft, lustrous black eyes' (301), to do the job properly. Alexandra's admission that '"Our lives are like the years, all made up of weather and crops and cows"' (131) exposes Cather's need to spice things up. At the same time she is clearly doubtful about the credibility of the relationship and, in a rather desperate bid to pre-empt criticism, she even allows the lovers to comment on what a very dull affair theirs is: '"Are you the least bit disappointed in our coming together?" [Carl] asked abruptly' (131).

It is hard to imagine what on earth could disturb the course of a love so placid but Cather contrives to have Lou and Oscar bear down on Carl, in case any of Alexandra's property should escape them, and as the imputation of fortune hunting is too much for him, he slinks off, remarking, '"It is your fate to be always surrounded by little men"' (181). His hopes dashed, he goes off to be a 'dreamer' (301) on the Klondike. By this ploy Cather can spin out the empty dramatic thread until the end of the novel: Carl pops up again, within minutes everything is '"just as it used to be"' (303) and they marry. Their relationship is contrived; worked into the novel as a sop to the conventions, in deference to prevailing literary expectations.

Carl returns in Part II, not only for romantic reasons, but to enable Cather to debate the merits of life in the East and West. When the Linstrum family decide to leave the farm, Alexandra is disappointed for herself but glad for Carl. She has the pioneer's love of the land but he is an artist and must go East. When he comes to visit her sixteen years later, she observes that 'he had not become a trim, self-satisfied city man' (115); a remark which betrays the Westerner's distrust of urban sophistication. Carl's arrival provokes a variety of responses. Lou and Oscar are suspicious and Lou, in particular, is belligerently anti-Eastern. He wants to dynamite Wall Street and insists that the West is going to make itself heard. Annie Lee, on the contrary, is anxious for the West not to seem backward and uncouth and talks loudly about her new dining room furniture. The family, then, express the range of Western envy and resentment of the East; a sense both of moral superiority and cultural inadequacy.

Between Alexandra and Carl the issue is debated at yet greater length. He has not become an artist; he touches up photographs and produces cheap engravings. Life in the city is synonymous to him with artificiality and pretence. Alexandra's prosperity is contrasted with his poverty: '"I couldn't buy even one of your cornfields"' (122). But she still believes in his way of life; '"I'd rather have had your freedom than my land"' (122). He counters with a litany of the evils of city life; the anonymity and loneliness. For her though, the rootlessness and obscurity are outweighed by breadth of vision. The West is monotonous and narrow: '"If the world were no wider than my cornfields, if there were not something besides this, I wouldn't feel that it was worth much to work"' (124).

Her hopes are centred on her younger brother, Emil. Unlike Alexandra, who had to work to survive, and Carl, who went East in poverty, Emil has a '"whole chance"' (117). She can afford to send him to university and feels that all her hard years are vindicated in the opportunities they have afforded him. She is gratified that he has 'a personality apart from the soil' (213) but in fact he is motiveless and confused. Emil is a prototype of Claude Wheeler in *One of Ours*, one of Cather's 'Hamlets of the Plains'; discontented, introspective, lost. He suffers from a kind of cultural schizophrenia; he has lost touch with his past and finds himself unable to engage in the present. Alexandra says of him: '"On the outside Emil is just like an American boy . . . but underneath he is more Swedish than any of us"' (117).

When Emil is killed, Alexandra's hopes are utterly destroyed. (Emil has an affair with Marie Shabata. He and Marie are murdered by her husband, Frank.) Alexandra visits Frank in prison and is filled with a sense of tragic waste, not only on her brother's account but on Frank's. She is bitter and disillusioned, but the catastrophe which precipitates her despair is so contrived, it is difficult to feel much sympathy. The element of melodrama in the double murder is emphasised by her quotation from Byron's somewhat histrionic poem, 'The Prisoner of Chillon': 'Henceforth the world will only be/A wider prison-house to me, –' (298). It is surely completely out of character for Alexandra, so very sensible and straightforward, to adopt the pose of a disillusioned Romantic and walk the streets of Lincoln overcome with 'disgust of life' (298).

The journey to the New World, then, results in disaster for Frank, Emil and Marie and terrible unahppiness for Alexandra. And even success brings family division and tension, with Lou and Oscar squabbling over money and so ashamed of their immigrant origins that they never speak Swedish in public. The pioneer experience hardly proves felicitous for any of them and Alexandra, remembering her father's dream for their future, hopes '"that he is among the old people of his blood and country, and that tidings do not reach him from the New World"' (183). And yet *O Pioneers!* ends triumphantly: 'Fortunate country that is one day to receive hearts like Alexandra's into its bosom, to give them out again in the yellow wheat, in the rustling corn, in the shining eyes of youth!' (309). After so much death and despair it is difficult to see how such ecstatic optimism can be justified. Emil's history certainly could not have led the narrator to this conclusion. Nor, as the pinnacle of Alexandra's pioneering hopes, would his life warrant a belief in the superiority of the West. None the less, at the end of the book Cather comes down suddenly and heavily on the Western side. Although previously Alexandra had said to Carl of his life in New York '"I'd rather have had your freedom than my land"', the evaluation is reversed here and it is decided they will stay on the farm: '"There is great peace here Carl, and freedom . . ." Alexandra took a deep breath and looked off into the red west' (307).

Cather's self-consciousness is evident in a conceit which runs from Part II onward and is first voiced by Carl. He and Alexandra are remembering the old days when the graveyard was wild prairie and he remarks: '"Isn't it queer: there are only two or three human stories, and they go on repeating themselves as fiercely as if they had never happened before"', (119). It is hardly a brilliant tactical move for a writer to admit that hers is an old story which has been told before and that the repetition, however passionate, may prove tedious. Part I is an original story of the pioneers and Cather was on firm if untrodden ground; what ensues is conventional novel material told in the conventional way. Of the two or three stories available, Cather opted for the rather thin one of how mature, sensible people get married and the racy one about star-crossed lovers – with a dash of adultery. The latter is perhaps intended to compensate for the blandness of the former. When Cather writes of Alexandra, 'Her mind was a white book, with clear writing about weather and beasts and growing things. Not many people would have cared to read it, only a happy few' (205), anybody who finds Alexandra's love affair a trifle dull may consider themselves soundly snubbed if not morally deficient. Yet Cather's superior tone here is less complacent than defensive.

Alexandra's story is rather clinically wholesome; Emil and Marie's is dark and stormy. Although their affair and

Frank's jealousy are sensitively treated there is no doubt that it has all been done before. It is self-conscious and literary; like the conventional romance of local colour. At the end, Cather attempts to minimise the element of melodrama by narrating the murders indirectly. The device of having Ivar discover the bodies and deduce the events is clever but highly artificial; the ingenuity is so evident that it inhibits any sense of tragedy or even pathos. The reader is aware that Cather is spinning a yarn: 'The story of what happened was written plainly in the orchard grass, and on the white mulberries that had fallen in the night and were covered in dark stain' (268). The metaphor continues, 'For Emil the chapter had been short' (269), and apparently even develops, 'But the stained, slippery grass, the darkened mulberries, told only half the story' (270). The other half is told through a rather precious image of 'two white butterflies . . . fluttering in and out among the interlacing shadows.' The story conceit is finally laid to rest at the end of the novel when Carl and Alexandra are reunited and she has become reconciled to her brother's death: '"You remember what you once said about . . . the old story writing itself over? Only it is we who write it, with the best we have"' (307). But these references to life as a fiction, only serve to underline the artificiality of Cather's portrayal.

One striking feature of *O Pioneers!* is its Russian flavour. Although the subject is quintessentially American, the style owes something to Turgenev and, to a lesser extent, to Tolstoy. The descriptions of ordinary rural life, for example, often recall the tone and atmosphere of Turgenev's *Sketches from a Hunter's Album*. It is an aspect of style which is difficult to define but which belongs to writers' attitudes to their material. Turgenev's careful observation and deep affection for the Russian countryside, which emerge in the descriptions of 'Forest and Steppe', 'Yermolay and the Miller's Wife' and 'Bezhin Lea', find their counterpart in *O Pioneers!*. To both writers the land has a personality of its own which profoundly affects the narrators as they respond emotionally to its appeal. But for Cather the absence of history and identity made a model imperative and so she turned to the Russians. Moreover, Turgenev, unlike American local colourists, had a breadth of education and understanding which ensured that he never became narrowly provincial. Cather commented on this as early as 1895:

> The great artists, like Turgeneff, have always used [local colour] with an almost niggardly care. There are places in Turgeneff's novels where you can fairly feel him restraining from assisting himself by sombre Russian landscapes and the threadbare, pathetic Russian peasant.[18]

Turgenev specialises not only in threadbare but in wise peasants. Cather's Crazy Ivar could have come straight out of Turgenev; indeed his prototype can be found in 'Kasyan from the Beautiful Lands' in the *Sketches*.[19] Like Kasyan, Ivar is a kind of holy fool, living alone in a clay bank, 'his shaggy white hair, falling in a thick mane about his ruddy cheeks' (37); walking barefoot is his only sensual indulgence. Kasyan is renowned locally for his herbal remedies; he considers shooting game a sin and prefers to tramp through the countryside rather than stay at home, because when '"the sweet sunlight shines on you"', you are '"clearer to God"' (93). Ivar doctors sick animals, forbids shooting, and lives in a remote part of the country because 'his Bible seemed truer to him there' (38). Ivar's importance in the novel is as a representative of the Old World in a community that is shedding its customs and beliefs as fast as it can and despises what Alexandra calls the '"old time"' (95) people and ways. He is a spokesman for the values which are cherished in the work of Turgenev and Tolstoy and denigrated in America. As Ivar says, '"The way here is for all to do the alike"' (92). Only Alexandra's protection keeps him from being locked up in an asylum.

In 1922 Cather wrote a very important letter to H. L. Mencken in which she discussed the impact of Russian writing on her early work. She outlines what she was trying to achieve in *O Pioneers!* and why her West was different from that of other Western writers. She begins by confessing that she has often had a deep inner toothache of the soul, wondering whether she was unconsciously copying some 'foreign' writer. She tells how when *O Pioneers!* was written it was a terribly lonesome book; she couldn't find any other that left out the usual story machinery. She wonders whether her mind had got a kink put in it by the four shorter (*sic*) novels of Tolstoy – *Anna Karenina, The Cossacks, The Death of Ivan Illych* and *The Kreuzer Sonata* which, in indifferent English, fell into her hands when she was fourteen. She used to wonder whether they had so marked her that she couldn't see the American scene as it looked to other Americans. She says that 'The White Mulberry Tree' and 'O Pioneers!' (first draft), the nucleus from which it was made, were written before her first, artificial novel (*Alexander's Bridge*) but she did not show them to a publisher. She concludes by explaining that because their pattern was so different, she thought they must be the artificial ones, real only to her because she had a romantic and lyric attachment for the country about which they were written.[20]

Cather rather overestimates *O Pioneers!'* lack of artificiality but the connection she makes between 'foreign' writers and her individual perception of America is vital. What is surprising is that she singles out Tolstoy as the one who most influenced her. The letter is odd: she is curiously specific in the mention of Tolstoy's novels but vague as to their effect. As *War and Peace* is excluded one can assume that she was not influenced by his religious or historical preoccupations nor, having read him in poor translations, could she have intended any specific use

of language. It is also strange that she should identify
Tolstoy with the absence of the usual story machinery
in *O Pioneers!*, as his novels are all plot structured to a
greater or lesser degree. Such an absence recalls rather the
loose, anecdotal form of Turgenev's *Sketches*.

It was Tolstoy's Russianness to which she really
responded; the pastoral aspect of his genius. In a letter
of 1924 Cather states that the two authors in modern times
she admires most are Tolstoy and Turgenev[21]: their appeal
for her can be found in their special feeling for landscape
and their sympathy with the peasantry and folklore; in
short, a romantic and lyric attachment to their country.
Given this, it is strange that Cather should have cited
Tolstoy; his massiveness, weight, and the tendency of his
characters to indulge in metaphysical speculation, make him
inappropriate to her. Turgenev's delicacy, and the fact that
for him social and political concerns are always secondary,
make her closer to him and yet he is, as it were, specifically
not mentioned. Cather told Mencken that he could use her
letter when he wrote her obituary and the reason why she
cited Tolstoy may be because he is universally acknowledged to be a great writer, whereas Turgenev's reputation,
rightly or wrongly, is considerably slighter. As I have tried
to show, Cather was concerned that being designated a
local colourist would detract from her achievement, but by
having her name yoked with the Count's, no one could say
her work was feminine and small. Unfortunately, however
handy Cather hoped it might prove, Mencken never availed
himself of the information she sent him.

In *O Pioneers!* 'foreign' influence is not fully assimilated.
Indeed, the novel is comprised of undigested elements without ever fully achieving a unified vision. It marks a pivotal
moment in Cather's career. She need not follow Wharton
and James but could return to her own country without
the fear of being peripheral and insignificant. The Russians
provided her with models for local colour that were neither

folksy nor quaint; which could deal with a range of human relations and a depth of emotion which even the work of Sarah Orne Jewett, America's most sensitive and intelligent local colourist, had not come near to achieving. Cather could give to Western literature what it had hitherto lacked – depth and breadth – through her profound love and her knowledge that 'the world was wider than [her] cornfields'.

With this novel Cather began to tell the story of the West as she herself had known it. But to do so she did not feel that she had to reject all the literature that had gone before. Unlike Garland and Anderson she did not imagine that to be authentically American one must maintain the kind of pristine Western individuality which Anderson, for example, displays in *A Story Teller's Story*. He recounts how he was often accused of imitating the Russians and credited, through their influence, with bringing 'the American peasant into literature'. Having read this so often, he tells us, he decided to read a little and discovered that in Russian novels people are always eating cabbage soup, he has no doubt Russian writers eat it too, he himself was 'raised largely on cabbage soup', so he reckons the critics are right.[22] Although Anderson's flippancy is amusing, his somewhat fatuous response to Russian literature illustrates the fundamental difference between Cather and the majority of her Western contemporaries.

Cather was prepared to look to Europe and to learn from it. Art does not happen in a vacuum and the American call for new forms, entailed for Cather, taking the old forms and making them hers. She could not have agreed with Whitman's Pioneers: 'All the past we leave behind.'[23] For her, a land without history could never have a literature of its own. Without the past there were no values, no art, no culture. The New World was peopled by the Old and it was by writing of the European immigrant that Cather could tell the story of the Midwest. In *O Pioneers!* America's European heritage is like an unfinished jigsaw puzzle; all the pieces are there but not the picture. It was a Virgilian perspective of the pioneers as exiles, bringing their gods with them to found a new civilisation, which gave Cather her vision of the Midwest. It is this vision which is at the heart of *My Ántonia* and gives it unity and coherence: she, like Virgil, would bring the Muse into her country.

# 4 The golden girl of the West:

*My Ántonia*

Horace Greely's famous injunction, 'Go West young man and grow up with the country' is obeyed to the letter by Jim Burden, the narrator of *My Ántonia*. Indeed, the novel's opening deliberately sets a false trail evoking the world of cowboys, saloons and campfires and encouraging the reader to expect a conventional Western adventure. Jim Burden, recently orphaned, and Jake Marpole, 'a mountain boy', are on their way from Virginia to Jim's grandparents in Nebraska 'to try [their] fortunes in a new world' (3). To underline the point Cather even has Jim reading a 'Life of Jesse James' on his train journey West. Glued to his dime novel, Jim declines to meet the Bohemian girl and her family, also travelling to Black Hawk, and is backed up by Jake who said 'you were likely to get diseases from foreigners' (5). The novel, it seems, is to inhabit the white, male, Protestant sphere of the classic Western.

On his arrival at the station Jim is met by the Burden's hired man, Otto Fuchs, whose greeting seems to promise all the excitement of the wild frontier: '"Hello, Jimmy, ain't you scared to come so far west?"' Jim, on the contrary, is delighted to find reality apparently conforming so closely to fictional stereotype:

> [Fuchs] might have stepped out of the pages of 'Jesse James'. He wore a sombrero hat, with a wide leather

band and a bright buckle, and the ends of his moustache were twisted up stiffly, like little horns. He looked lively and ferocious, I thought, as if he had a history. A long scar ran across one cheek and drew the corner of his mouth up in a sinister curl. The top of his left ear was gone, and his skin was brown as an Indian's. Surely this was the face of a desperado. (6)

They pile into a wagon covered in buffalo hide and continue their journey through the night, into the realms of Western lawlessness: 'I had the feeling that the world was left behind, that we had got over the edge of it, and were outside man's jurisdiction' (7). At the end of this odyssey Jim is bathed, fed and put to bed by his grandmother. Without having to resort to broad parody, Cather undermines the Western myth with humour and gentle irony. The novel's opening is part of this subversive scheme and, as the narrative progresses, Jim's expectations are completely overturned: in the end his West is not that of Jesse James, the hero is not an American but a foreigner, not a cowboy but a young girl, and even the cowboy is not a gun-toting desperado but an Austrian Catholic whose scars are only the marks of his struggle to survive in a new country.

In the first sections Cather plays with the stereotypes of the macho West. The saloon, for example, is run by the sober and intelligent Anton Jelinek and is a 'respectable' (217) place where the immigrant farmers eat their lunch when they drive into town. Or again, the unmarried Western male who never launders or cooks anything but beans, is found 'batching' (36) in *My Ántonia*. The Russians, Peter and Pavel, are thoroughly domestic: Peter washes their clothes, keeps a cow and cooks cucumbers in the milk.

There are no shoot-outs and no lynchings and the only 'Western' adventure is mock-heroic. The time Jim and Ántonia are attacked by a rattler becomes a typical 'tall tale' which Ántonia's children are still telling at the end of the book. Although the mature narrator realises that the snake was old and lazy, Ántonia is deeply impressed when Jim kills it: '"You is just like big mans . . . Nobody ain't seen in this kawn-tree so big snake like you kill"' (46). And her admiration has a gratifying effect: 'The great land had never looked to me so big and free. If the red grass were full of rattlers, I was equal to them all' (48). Unlike the typical Western hero, however, this is the first and last time that Jim's masculine prowess is called upon.

But Cather's most important subversion of stereotype occurs in the portrait of Otto Fuchs. He has been a stage-driver, a cow-puncher, a miner and has all the trappings: 'He got out his 'chaps' and silver spurs to show them to Jake and me, and his best cowboy boots, with tops stitched in bold design – roses and true-lover's knots, and undraped female figures. These, he solemnly explained, were angels' (13). As he sits with the family on Saturday nights, popping corn and singing 'Bury me not on the Lone Prairie' and 'For I Am a Cowboy and Know I've Done Wrong', he appears simple and innocent without being sentimentalised. There is, admittedly, a touch of Owen Wister's nostalgia for the noble cowboy in Jim's memory of Jake and Otto: 'I can see the sag of their tired shoulders against the whitewashed wall. What good fellows they were, how much they knew, and how many things they had kept faith with!' Unlike Wister's upwardly mobile Virginian, Jake and Otto 'never get on, somehow' (68). When the Burdens move to town Otto decides to return to what he called the 'Wild West' and he is last heard of at the Yankee Girl Mine. Otto's drifting existence follows the conventional pattern of the cowboy but his European origin and his Catholic faith are an innovation. The significance of this will emerge later, I hope, but first it is necessary to explore how Cather's interest in Europe affected her vision of the West.

Cather created the first spaghetti Western: it was Virgil who provided her with the perspective on her past that enabled *My Ántonia* to be written. As I outlined in the previous chapter, there were two primary difficulties for the literature of the Midwest to overcome: the fact that it was a new country without history, tradition or associations and the related problem of form. Virgil had faced fundamentally similar obstacles some two thousand years before. To take the first point, as L. P. Wilkinson points out in his introduction to the *Georgics*, Virgil's Italy was a recent phenomenon: 'The *Georgics* celebrates a land that had been united politically only two generations previously . . . in 89 B.C..'[1] Nebraska had been formally made a State and accepted into the Union in 1867, less than two generations before the publication of *My Ántonia*.

To a great extent, then, the Romans of Virgil's day had no mythology, any more than Americans had in Cather's. The only body of literature available to the Romans was Greek – as the Americans only had English – with the consequent danger of producing imitative, second-rate art. In his essay on 'The Originality of the *Aeneid*'[2] Brooks Otis maintains that Roman history could not be turned into poetry because it 'wholly lacked the poetical images, the poetical cosmos without which, at that time, no poet could function.' In creating his national epic, Virgil had no choice but to commandeer Homer and take the Greek epics of the *Odyssey* and the *Iliad* as his models: 'The system of the *Aeneid* – is homerically worked out, largely because there was no Roman system or mythology, no Roman 'heroic age' that was at all usable. There were no gods and heroes but Homer's gods and heroes.'

The myths of the Greek heroic age provided Virgil with what Otis terms 'a symbology' and a structure; the first half of the *Aeneid* is an 'inversion' of the *Odyssey*, the second half is patterned on the *Iliad*. According to Otis, Virgil's radical innovation lay, not in creating a new myth or poetic form, but in adapting the existing one:

> The fact that myth – and *in concreto* the myth of the Greek heroic age – was the traditional subject of poetry, that the two indeed were indissolubly united, was a *datum* that Virgil took from Greek literature and could not alter. But Greek and Latin poets before Virgil generally interpreted this *datum* as a limit rather than as a positive source of ideas.

Just as in America there was a feeling that the old European forms were exhausted and in any case inappropriate to a new, American experience, so for the Romans Homeric myth seemed not only 'used up' but out of date. A Roman hero, to take but one example, needed very different qualities to survive from a swashbuckling Achilles or Odysseus, but Virgil saw the possibility of transforming the old type while still retaining the heroic stature.

Virgil attempted to 'retain the evocative or poetic power' of the Homeric myth while wholly changing its 'application'. Thus he could write new history in an old form. Cather, too, was original in this sense, seeing that European models could be 'inverted' and adapted to fit a new context. Virgil reversed the *nostos*, for example, making Aeneas travel away from home not towards it, in the same way Cather inverted the conventional pattern of the novel, saying of *My Ántonia* that it was just 'the other side of the rug'.[3]

One could not say, of course, that Cather actually modelled *My Ántonia* on any one particular book of Virgil's. Although critics often refer to it as a pastoral, invariably all that is intended by this is a rural story with a happy ending. Indeed, pastoral is levelled almost as an accusation, carrying with it the connotation of escapism and evasion of reality. But pastoral is not , strictly, appropriate to Cather. It refers to certain Idylls of Theocritus and Virgil's *Eclogues*, or *Bucolics* as they are also known, which were based on the Greek. From there came the English pastoral tradition of Spenser, Sidney, Milton and so on. Pastoral poetry is concerned with shepherds and their life and loves; it contains formal set pieces such as the poetry and singing competitions and was intended to portray idealised scenes of rustic life for a sophisticated city reading public.

In his essay 'Arcadia on the Range',[4] James E. Phillips makes a case for the re-emergence of pastoral in the American West. Substitute cattle for sheep, and cowboys for shepherds, and the songs of Theocritus turn into 'Home on the Range'. Phillips identifies certain key features of pastoral, particularly the Renaissance pastoral exemplified by Sidney's *Arcadia*, in Western literature: the contrast between a simple rural life and the complexities of urban existence, the use of Arcadia as a means of criticising the corruption of the city, the clear moral universe in which virtue always triumphs and an aristocracy based on innate goodness not social caste. Phillips finds these distinguishing traits in Owen Wister's *The Virginian*, where the hero and heroine are anything but proletarian, villainy is always defeated, and there is the kind of deliberate artificiality which ensured that Western pastoral had nothing to do with the historical West.[5]

Cather's work is not pastoral in this sense and *My Ántonia* has less to do with the *Eclogues* than the *Georgics*. In these, Virgil followed another Greek, the peasant poet Hesiod and his *Works and Days*, which deals with farming life, particularly growing crops, and which sings the praise of dung rather than shepherdesses. It is a practical and moral work addressed to a farmer not an urban reader. Virgil, too, though less didactic than descriptive, retained Hesiod's emphasis on the value of hard work and rustic virtue. The *Georgics* presents a panorama of rural life: descriptions of the seasons and the occupations appropriate to each, of country festivals and rites, instructions for the propagation of trees, the tending of animals and, throughout, an expression of the dignity of agricultural labour. Virgil's particular range of subject matter in the *Georgics*, and his blend of harsh realism with poetry, must have been attractive to Cather.

Virgil also provided Cather with a perspective on the European immigrant in America. Through the *Aeneid's* story of a dispossessed people founding a civilisation in a new land, Cather could endow the immigrant with epic stature. They were no longer a motley assortment, strewn across a continent but a people with an almost divinely inspired purpose. Ántonia, for example, is described as having a 'special mission' (367). She is not just a Bohemian serving girl or a 'battered woman' but, surrounded by her children, 'She was a rich mine of life, like the founders of early races' (353). The *Aeneid* could confer dignity on the immigrants: their sod houses and makeshift arrangements had seemed merely squalid but placed in an epic context, the Shimerdas eating prairie dog (first cousin to the rat), becomes not disgusting but heroic, akin to the hunger and privation endured by Aeneas and his crew. The *Aeneid*, too, is a poem about loss, struggle, defeat and only final success. The Trojans suffer not only physical hardship but most of all from a sense of isolation and exile; the same quality of loneliness and longing for the old country which Cather saw in the immigrant and which gave such pathos to their settling of America.

Although Cather did not base *My Ántonia* on the *Aeneid* in any exact way, there are parallels, of recurring themes and motifs, and events which have the same symbolic function. For example, the theme of exile, which persists even after the Trojans arrive in Italy, is given its most dramatic expression by the burning of the boats in Book V. Many of the women, still inconsolable at the loss of Troy, are tempted by the easier prospect of settling in Sicily with Acestes, instead of pressing on to Latium to found the new civilisation. In the same way, in *My Ántonia* there

are some who do not have the strength to be pioneers
and give up the struggle. Unlike Virgil, however, Cather
does not portray this as an exclusively female trait. It is Mr
Shimerda who cannot endure the loss of the old country and
the conditions in the new. His suicide is the expression of
the pioneer's unbearable sense of exile; the counterpart of
the burning of the boats, in a more tragic vein.

Mr Shimerda has another important function in the
novel, similar to Anchises, Aeneas's father, who serves
as a reminder to the Trojans of their destiny. In the
same way, Mr Shimerda represents Old World culture,
sensitivity and integrity to the immigrants. Although,
like Anchises, he dies early in the story he transmits
these values to his daughter and to Jim Burden, who
both feel for him a Virgilian sense of *pietas*, or filial
piety. It is because of him that the old culture, like
the household gods the Trojans carry with them to Italy,
is not forgotten in America. Anchises' function is most
clearly realised in Book VI when Aeneas meets his father
in the Underworld. Aeneas says that it is Anchises' memory
which has helped him to survive: '"Your image, it
was, your troubled phantom/That, often rising before
me, has brought me to this place"' to hear of his
destiny and the future of Rome.[6] It is Aeneas's filial
piety for Anchises which strengthens his resolve, enables
him to surmount hardship and settle in Italy.

In *My Ántonia* there is a lengthy passage of reflection
after Mr Shimerda's suicide. Cather's prosaic, unemotional
portrayal of the death – a corpse found in the barn, the
congealed, frozen blood – and particularly the way in
which death is unaccented, simply part of a stream of
events, has often been remarked upon. But in between
the practicalities of coffin making and the difficulty of
finding a burial ground, there is a strange interlude in
which Jim, left alone at home, imagines Mr Shimerda's
ghost. The passage functions very much in the same way

as Aeneas's visit to the Underworld. Jim thinks that Mr Shimerda's spirit may stop to rest at his house on its way back to Bohemia: 'Surely, his exhausted spirit, so tired of cold and crowding and the struggle with the ever-falling snow, was resting now in this quiet house.' Like Aeneas meeting Anchises, Jim encounters the dead man:

> It was as if I had let the old man in out of the tormenting winter, and were sitting there with him . . . Such vivid pictures came to me that they might have been Mr. Shimerda's memories, not yet faded out from the air in which they had haunted him. (101–102)

The episode stays in Jim's mind, instilling in him a sense of filial piety, and as with Aeneas it changes, or rather confirms, the course of his life.

The related theme of nostalgia found in the *Aeneid* is also of considerable importance to *My Ántonia*. In book III, for example, Aeneas meets Andromache and Helenus. Still grieving for Hector, she and Helenus build an imitation Troy and indulge in lachrymose memories of former glory. Aeneas, not being a Homeric hero, but a sensitive, easily discouraged man could well fall victim to such nostalgia and remain with them. On arriving at Carthage in Book I he enters Dido's temple to Juno. In it he sees depicted scenes from the fall of Troy and is deeply moved: 'Tears in the nature of things, hearts touched by human transience' (line 462). Aeneas weeps for the passing of time and the frailty of all things. But, because this sensitivity is yoked to a feeling of filial piety, he does not lapse into mere nostalgia. Rather, nostalgia is transformed into a positive good, ensuring that the household gods will still be worshipped in Italy; that there will be a continuity of culture.

Mr Shimerda is associated with both the Virgilian concepts of *pietas* and *lacrimae rerum*, or pity of things. (The latter is perhaps particularly associated with the violin

which he no longer plays.) Reminders of the old country
continually come to the surface of *My Ántonia* and are often
connected with Mr Shimerda. Through their love for him,
Jim and Ántonia inherit his love of beauty. Looking closer,
one can see how this pattern of Virgilian references and
motifs draws many apparently disparate elements together,
countering the ubiquitous criticism that the novel is episodic
and formless. One of the earliest and most evocative of these
references also echoes Virgil's phrasing. One afternoon as
Jim and Ántonia are out walking they find a cricket. Its
'thin, rusty little chirp' (39) reminds Ántonia of a woman
called Old Hata, in Bohemia, who sold herbs and roots
and sang in a cracked voice. When they meet her father,
he listens to the faint chirp 'as if it were a beautiful sound':
'The old man's smile, as he listened, was so full of sadness,
of pity for things, that I never afterward forgot it' (42).

In the earlier parts of the book Jim is not always
so receptive. It is the retrospective narrator who values
the Shimerdas' memories and the treasures they carried
with them from the old country. When Mr Shimerda,
for example, intends to give Jim his curiously wrought
gun, Jim is simply relieved that the 'project was one
of futurity' (42). Or again, the mysterious flakes that
Mrs Shimerda unearths from a chest are sampled at
the time and unceremoniously thrown away:

> I never forgot the strange taste, though it was many years
> before I knew that those little brown shavings, which the
> Shimerdas had brought so far and treasured so jealously,
> were dried mushrooms. They had been gathered, prob-
> ably, in some deep Bohemian forest . . . (79)

Indeed, before Mr Shimerda's death, Jim is even occasionally contemptuous of the family's repeated preference
for the old 'kawn-tree' and for things '"like what you not
got here"' (42), and remarks chauvinistically: '"People

who don't like this country ought to stay at home . . .
We don't make them come here"' (89).

Mr Shimerda's suicide, though, changes Jim's perspective and establishes a bond between him and Ántonia. On
the day of the funeral she runs to him sobbing, '"Oh,
Jimmy . . . what you tink for my lovely papa!" It seemed
to me that I could feel her heart breaking as she clung to me'
(115). It confirms in both of them a feeling of filial piety:

'My father, he went much to school. He know a
great deal; how to make the fine cloth like what you
not got here. He play horn and violin, and he read so
many books that the priests in Bohemie come to talk
to him. You won't forget my father, Jim?'
'No,' I said, 'I will never forget him.'(124)

When Jim gives his 'surprisingly' good High School Commencement Speech, full of enthusiasm and fervour, Ántonia
and Jim are again united in the memory of her father:

'Oh, I just sat there and wished my papa could hear
you! Jim' – Ántonia took hold of my coat lapels
– 'there was something in your speech that made
me think so about my papa!'
'I thought about your papa when I wrote my speech,
Tony,' I said, 'I dedicated it to him.' (230–231)

Shortly after this, Jim begins reading Virgil, memorising
long passages of the *Aeneid*. It is as if Mr Shimerda not only
inspires him with a veneration for art, but specifically leads
him to Virgil. The summer Jim spends reading the *Aeneid*
out loud on his own in Black Hawk inspires in him a love
for his own country too, for Nebraska, which he conceives
in epic terms. It is a prefiguration of Tom Outland's
summer on the Blue Mesa in *The Professor's House* which
Tom spends, like Jim, committing the *Aeneid* to memory.

Outland, too, finds in Virgil an expression of love for a country which is close to his own. Tom's sense of *pietas* is toward the Indian past; their houses, pottery and tools reveal an early civilisation that lengthens America's past. In a similar way in *One of Ours*, Claude feels a sense of obligation, but in his case to America's European forebears. He sails on a troop ship, bound for France during the First World War, called the *Anchises*, suggesting a parallel with the myth of Aeneas carrying his father on his back after the fall of Troy. Through Virgil, then, America could look to its native, Indian heritage and the European civilisation of the people who had come to settle it.

The epic framework of *My Ántonia* is achieved through Jim's perception of his neighbours. Even when the references do not come directly from Virgil their cumulative effect is to support the epic perspective on the pioneers. Mr Shimerda, for example, is likened to Coronado, whom Jim is convinced came through Nebraska in search of the Seven Golden Cities, and who '"died in the wilderness of a broken hear"' (244). In the middle of winter, in the deep snow, the hired men who work in the fields all day seem to Jim like 'Arctic explorers' (65–66). Ántonia has a 'special mission'. Fuchs, too, who appears to Jim at first like the archetypal cowboy, is incorporated in the Virgilian scheme.

The Christmas when the family is snowed in and cannot buy provisions is saved by Otto. The family make candles and gingerbread animals to decorate the tree, 'its real splendours, however, came from the most unlikely place in the world – from Otto's cowboy trunk': 'he now produced a collection of brilliantly coloured paper figures, several inches high and stiff enough to stand alone. They had been sent to him year after year by his old mother in Austria' (83). With the three kings, camels, leopards and a manger, the tree 'became like the talking tree of the fairy tale . . . Grandmother said it reminded her of the Tree of Knowledge.' The carefully preserved paper figures are reminders of customs and rituals from the old country. And once the candles are lit, the tree suddenly acquires a more precise religious significance: it is adorned with Otto's household gods. Mr Shimerda even crosses himself and kneels down before it but with a religious tolerance, characteristic of Virgil, 'Grandfather merely put his finger-tips to his brow and bowed his venerable head, thus Protestantizing the atmosphere' (87).

The particular significance of Virgil to *My Ántonia* emerges most clearly in Book III, 'Lena Lingard', when Jim is studying at Lincoln University. It has often been objected that Lena Lingard occupies too much space in a novel entitled *My Ántonia;* that she is irrelevant or at best unrelated. But Lena, as I hope will become apparent, is an integral part of the novel's Virgilian design. In Books I and II Jim grows up with the country, in Books IV and V he returns to it, but Book III marks an important transitional stage, in which he harvests his youthful experience and gains the vision of life which shapes his narration of the past and thus the structure of the novel.

It opens with Jim, under the tutelage of Gaston Cleric, furthering his study of Virgil. In the course of several pages Cather gives us Jim's thoughts as he digests his Latin lessons. He begins with Dante's veneration for Virgil, for his 'sweet teacher', and he quotes the lines from the 'Commedia' of the poet Statius, who speaks for Dante; '"The seeds of my ardour were the sparks from that divine flame whereby more than a thousand have kindled; I speak of the 'Aeneid', mother to me and nurse to me in poetry"' (262). As the narrator of the novel, Jim 'speaks' for Cather. In the same way, the *Aeneid* is the mother of *My Ántonia;* it might even be said that the *Georgics* is the father.

Before examining these family connections, it is necessary to refer to one of the closing episodes of Book II. Jim and the hired girls are coming home at the end of the day from a picnic:

> On some upland farm, a plough had been left standing
> in a field. The sun was sinking just behind it. Magnified
> across the distance by the horizontal light, it stood
> out against the sun, was exactly contained within the
> circle of the disk; the handles, the tongue, the share
> – black against the molten red. There it was, heroic
> in size, a picture writing on the sun. (245)

The famous image of the plough against the sun is usually
understood as a symbol of the pioneers; of an heroic moment
in history which vanished all too soon:

> Even while we whispered about it, our vision dis-
> appeared; the ball dropped and dropped until the red
> tip went beneath the earth. The fields below us were
> dark, the sky was growing pale, and that forgotten
> plough had sunk back to its own littleness some-
> where on the prairie. (245)

It is, certainly, an image of fading glory and transience,
of melancholy, associated with Virgil's lament that the best
days are the first to flee, which Jim quotes in Book III.
But it is more than this – indeed, it is less a symbol of
the lost frontier than of the settlement of the West. It is
epic in scope; heralding, not the end of the pioneers, but
the beginning of a new civilisation. This is made clear
during one of Jim's ruminations on the *Aeneid*:

> While I was in the very act of yearning towards the
> new forms that Cleric brought up before me, my mind
> plunged away from me, and I suddenly found myself
> thinking of the places and people of my own infinitesimal
> past. They stood out strengthened and simplified now,
> like the image of the plough against the sun. (262)

Through his reading of Virgil, Jim makes sense of his
experience and gives it meaning: his 'own naked land and

the figures scattered upon it' are fixed in his memory and his 'infinitesimal past' is lengthened until at the end of the novel it becomes 'the precious, the incommunicable past' (372).

The image of the plough is also associated with the *Georgics*. Gaston Cleric had suggested that when Virgil was dying in Brindisi, and had faced the bitter fact that he was to leave the *Aeneid* unfinished,

> . . . his mind must have gone back to the perfect utterance of the 'Georgics,' where the pen was fitted to the matter as the plough is to the furrow, and he must have said to himself, with the thankfulness of a good man, 'I was the first to bring the Muse into my country.' (264)

The problems Western literature had to overcome – finding new forms, being a new country, not imitating English – are echoed in Cleric's lesson on Book III of the *Georgics*:

> '*Primus ego in patriam mecum . . . deducam Musas*' . . . [He] had explained that '*patria*' here meant, not a nation or even a province, but the little rural neighbourhood on the Mincio where the poet was born. This was not a boast, but a hope, at once bold and devoutly humble, that he might bring the Muse (but lately come to Italy from her cloudy Grecian mountains), not to the capital, the *palatio Romana*, but to his own little 'country' . . . (264)

And Cather wanted to bring the Muse (but lately come from Europe), not to New York and Boston, but to the little area around Red Cloud.

While in the middle of his reflections, Jim is unexpectedly interrupted by a call from Lena Lingard. She is radiant and relaxed and brings news of the other hired girls. When she leaves, Jim has what appears to some, a surprising revelation:

When I closed my eyes I could hear them all laughing –
the Danish laundry girls and the three Bohemian Marys.
Lena had brought them all back to me. It came over me,
as it had never done before, the relation between girls like
those and the poetry of Virgil. If there were no girls like
them in the world, there would be no poetry. (270)

In his essay 'Willa Cather: The Classic Voice',[7] Donald
Sutherland remarks on the strangeness of this 'relation',
being utterly baffled by the association of Virgil with girls.
As Sutherland says, Virgil was not a love poet and, with
the exception of Dido and Aeneas, never strayed into the
realms of romantic passion. But this is precisely part of
Virgil's appeal for Cather for she too wanted to explore
themes and directions other than the amorous or domestic.
Jim's feeling for the Danish girls and the Bohemian Marys
is not primarily a romantic one. They and Lena represent
the best in the pioneers and epitomise the experiences of
his youth. They are, in the Virgilian sense, 'the country',
and their prominent position in the novel, far from being
a sign of formlessness, is absolutely necessary.

*My Ántonia*, then, may be read as a *Georgic* with epic
overtones. But it differs from Virgil in one important
respect in that its emphasis is female. Epic, and even
pastoral, is largely a male affair, but Cather focused her
attention on the pioneer women. Although the narrator is
male he is not in himself of paramount importance. He
exists – as a sympathetic involved narrator, informed with
a Virgilian perspective in order, largely, to evoke them.
And the fact that she chose a male narrator was simply
one of convenience; she said at the time that she had
no intention of 'writing like a man' but clearly she could
not have used a female narrator to describe the hired girls
without introducing irrelevant complications.[8]

Ántonia, of course, is the most compelling of Cather's
'jeunes filles en fleur' but she is only one of a group. Indeed

there is a kind of female network in the novel with the connections between families, and the relations between the generations, being maintained largely by the women. When Jim arrives in Nebraska, for example, it is his grandmother with whom he establishes a relationship; his grandfather remaining always a distantly impressive figure, benignly patriarchal. Mrs Burden is domestic, capable, humorous and frank: 'a strong woman, of unusual endurance' (11). It is she who visits the Shimerdas, takes the provisions, and when Ántonia later comes to town, Mrs Burden finds her a job with Mrs Harling. The young Bohemian and the middle-aged Norwegian suit each other very well: 'There was a basic harmony between Ántonia and her mistress. They had strong, independent natures, both of them . . . They loved children and animals and music, and rough play and digging in the earth' (180). They are powerful figures who dominate without being dogmatic.

Frances Harling is a pioneer woman in a different way. She is in partnership with her father and the two of them 'discuss grain-cars and cattle, like two men' (150). She knows all the farming families in the area and feels an almost maternal concern for them; her interest 'was more than a business interest. She carried them all in her mind as if they were characters in a book or a play'. She often steps in to save them from the unscrupulous money lender, Wick Cutter. The important role played by women in the life of the community is underlined when Ántonia falls into social disgrace; only the Widow Steavens befriends her and it is she who tells Jim, Ántonia's story.

The immigrant girls relate to the older women in a social scheme which is both Virgilian and matriarchal: '[They] learned so much from life, from poverty, from their mothers and grandmothers; they had all, like Ántonia, been early awakened and made observant by coming at a tender age from an old country to a new' (198). The girls feel particularly the older women's sense of exile. Tiny Soderball hopes her

mother will not feel so 'homesick' since they began growing
rye; Anna takes home canned fish for her rambling grandmother who '"thinks she's at home in Norway"' (239);
Lena works so that her mother can move out of the sod
house, knowing that '"the men will never do it"' (241).

Respectable Black Hawk looks down on them as ignorant foreigners who are in service but it is because the
girls work and remain loyal to their families that their
farms do better than their neighbours'. Jim's partisan
narration trumpets their success:

> I always knew I should live long enough to see my
> country girls come into their own, and I have. To-day the
> best that a harassed Black Hawk merchant can hope for is
> to sell provisions and farm machinery and automobiles to
> the rich farms where that first crop of stalwart Bohemian
> and Scandinavian girls are now the mistresses. (201)

Part of Black Hawk's fear stems from the hired girls' looser
'morality'. Tiny Soderball, working at the hotel, flirts with
the travelling salesmen; Lena has a series of lovers; while
the three Bohemian Marys 'were the heroines of a cycle of
scandalous stories' (202) and are considered 'as dangerous
as high explosives' (203). The young men of the town would
rather dance with the fresh-smelling Danish girls who work
in the laundry than with their frigid classmates but though
the girls, as Ántonia says, are out to get their good
times while they can, they are not interested in catching
husbands. We do not hear each of their destinies but Tiny
remains unmarried, making a fortune in the Klondike;
Lena too remains single, prospering as a dressmaker, while
Ántonia marries from among her own people.

Lena's aversion is not to men but to marriage, pro-
viding an interesting contrast with Ántonia. Lena has
a very attractive character: practical and sensuous – a
waltz with Lena was like coming in with the tide – and

somehow perpetually innocent. Even as a smartly dressed townswoman she still seems like the cowgirl with white legs who unwittingly drove Ole Benson mad with desire. She is determined to become independent and to help her family but she has no intention of marrying: 'She remembered home as a place where there were always too many children, a cross man and work piling up around a sick woman' (291). In the end she lives comfortably, takes lovers when she chooses, and turns down all suitors for her hand: '"It's all being under somebody's thumb"' (292).

The hired girls' various destinies are all presented as equally valid. Whether they become farmers, prospectors or business women they are all pioneers. Cather neither judges nor prescribes: Lena's childlessness is not sterile, Ántonia's poverty is not failure. Ántonia is the most engaging and sympathetic of all Cather's creations. She is vividly brought to life through a series of scenes filtered through Jim's cherishing memory. She first appears as the pretty little Bohemian girl, unable to speak a word of English, and the object of her father's adoration. After his death she is set to work by her brother. She ploughs the fields and does heavy chores: 'the farm-hands around the country joked in a nasty way about it' (126). She brags about her strength and eats noisily 'like a man' (125). Sunburned and sweaty, clad in her dead father's boots, in the fields all day, Mrs Shimerda fears that '"she'll lose all her nice ways"' (125). She is determined that her family will prosper in the New World despite their poor start and is defensive at the least suggestion of being patronised. When Jim, for example, quotes his grandfather's weather forecast, Ántonia rudely remarks '"He not Jesus"' (121).

She is seen next in more propitious circumstances, working for the Harlings in Black Hawk. Here she sews, bakes, sings, tells stories and plays with the children. She is both in service and part of the family, without conflict, until the arrival of the dancing tent. After this she thinks of nothing but clothes and having her '"fling"' (208); she moves to the Cutter's house so that she will have more free time. Wick Cutter's attempted rape (Jim has been planted in Ántonia's bed to foil him) is as hilarious as anything in Mark Twain but it has sinister overtones for, despite her strength and intelligence, Ántonia's sexuality necessarily makes her vulnerable. Her seduction by the worthless Larry Donovan is not narrated directly. 'Poor Ántonia's' disgrace occurs while Jim is away. The events are narrated by the Widow Steavens with an almost Biblical resonance: '"She got her cattle home, turned them into the corral, and went into the house, into her room behind the kitchen, and shut the door. There, without calling to anybody, without a groan, she lay down on the bed and bore her child"' (316). Ántonia refuses to become pathetic or to be ashamed of her child, deliberately having her baby's photograph on display in the photographer's window in Black Hawk.

Her final manifestation is as the pioneer mother, married to Ánton Cuzak and presiding over her prodigious family. Jim delays visiting her, fearing that she will have become 'aged and broken' (328). The male disillusion on discovering that the beautiful girl next door has turned into a dull middle-aged housewife, which crops up with predictable regularity in fiction, is exposed here for all its sentimentality. It is one of the novel's crowning glories that though Ántonia is changed – practically toothless, even – she is still radiant: 'Ántonia came in and stood before me; a stalwart, brown woman, flat-chested, her curly brown hair a little grizzled . . . She was there in the full vigour of her personality, battered but not diminished' (331–332). With her children teeming around her on the bright, sunny farm, Ántonia has been described as an incarnation of Venus Genetrix.[9] But only Cather could create an earth mother with such an inconspicuous bust line.

Ántonia's household is a Bohemian one: Jim is offered coffee and *kolaches*, pictures of Prague hang on the parlour walls, the children cannot even speak English until they go to school. John J. Murphy in his essay 'The Virginian and Ántonia Shimerda' notes this, and relates it to the fact that Ántonia is seduced by an American and 'rescued by one of her own, Ánton Cuzak'. He refers to this as an '[understandable]' cultural reversion' and seems to feel that it requires some kind of apology or explanation: 'She inhabits an immigrant West opposed in many ways to the dominant culture, and identifies with the differences which have limited her.'[10] Cather, however, would certainly not have regarded the Old World heritage as a limiting factor – quite the reverse – for the novel is about the transplanting of European culture in American soil and repeatedly affirms Old World values. Moreover, the prospect of a 'dominant culture' is exactly what Cather objected to, fearing that it would amount to little more than bland conformity and standardisation. As I tried to show earlier, part of her intention in *My Ántonia* was precisely to show that there was an alternative to the prevailing 'white', male, Protestant mythology of the West.

Cather's ideal was an intermingling of Old and New; a rich, regional variety. When Jim, for example, makes a picture book for Yulka that snowy Christmas, he uses coloured pictures from cards he had 'brought from [his] "old country"', Virginia (81). What depressed Cather was the thought that the past – whether colonial or immigrant – could be lost, discarded in the race to get ahead, and that the distinctive customs of each area – born of the marriage of native geography and European settlement - could be obliterated in a vast sameness stretching from one end of America to the other. The 'conservatism' of her later years was really this: despair that the descendants of the Old World immigrants would trade in their household gods for automobiles.

Ántonia's life is, as Murphy suggests, limited: she could not go to school or marry one of Black Hawk's respectable citizens but she has an identity of her own, a language, beliefs and values. More importantly, she hands these on to her children who grow up both with an awareness of their national origins and fully able to take advantage of the opportunities in America. Ántonia on the farm, then, is not in retreat from Black Hawk. She inherits from her father and bequeaths to her own children the Virgilian love of old customs, rituals and beliefs; the continuity of the Old World in the New.

The transplanting of European culture to America is given a literal embodiment in a motif which occurs frequently in Cather's work: her immigrants are invariably to be found planting trees, protecting them from frost and watering them during the long hot summers. One can think of the Kohlers in *A Song of the Lark*, the Shabatas in *O Pioneers!*, or old Appelhof in *The Professor's House* and for all of them planting and tending has a Virgilian significance, both for its natural value (remembering the treatise on the propagation of trees in the *Georgics*) and as an act of reverence; a reminder of the distant homeland. It seems fitting that one of the final images of Ántonia should be in a garden and that it should be connected with her Virgilian 'mission' as the founder of a new civilisation:

> She had only to stand in the orchard, to put her hand on a little crab tree and look up at the apples, to make you feel the goodness of planting and tending and harvesting at last . . ..
>
> It was no wonder that her sons stood tall and straight. She was a rich mine of life, like the founders of early races. (353)

# 5 Time's fool and *A Lost Lady*

It is the difference between a remembered face and having that friend one day come in thru the door. She is really no more yours then than she has been right along in your memory.

Willa Cather Discusses Writing and Short Story Courses[1]

When Jim Burden writes *My Ántonia* on the cover of his manuscript, it is not an indication of possessiveness but an acknowledgement of the subjective nature of reality. Paradoxically, though the title *A Lost Lady* suggests a more objective account, the novel explores the limitations of perception, the failure to recognise that vision is always partial, and the distortions which this imposes. Marian Forrester is a very different heroine from any Cather had created before. Alexandra, Thea and Ántonia are all, to a greater or lesser extent, independent, assertive and relatively unambiguous; here, for the first time, Cather portrayed a female character who is vulnerable, capricious, complex and almost wholly reliant on masculine admiration. Men's eyes are the mirror in which she sees herself but they not only reflect, they can restrict and accuse or look the other way.

*A Lost Lady* has been seen by almost all Cather's critics as a lament for the passing of the old West and its values.[2] In this reading Marian Forrester is the flower of the pioneer age and her decline is a symbol of a society's disintegration under the corrupting influence of commercialism. Feminist critics have recently begun to challenge this view. Susan J. Rosowski, for example, argues that the novel is not an elegy for the pioneer past but an attempt to come to terms with the question of 'how to translate the best of the past into the present'. Kathleen L. Nichols has offered a pysochoanalytical interpretation in which she suggests that Niel's rejection of Mrs Forrester shows 'all the signs of a repressed oedipal conflict'; she is a 'lost lady' in his eyes but not in Cather's.[3]

That such conflicting readings should be possible is the result of Cather's complex narrative technique. She began in the first person, 'writing as the boy himself', but after several attempts she abandoned this mode and created a third-person narrator.[4] Niel's point of view remains central but it is framed within an omniscient narrative. Why, when she had written convincingly as Jim Burden in *My Ántonia*, did she feel that Niel's viewpoint alone was not adequate here? David Stouck, one of the few critics of the passing-of-the-West school to ponder this question at all, maintains that the double perspective 'allows for the introduction of an ironic perspective . . . through Niel we experience the attraction of Mrs. Forrester's style and charm, but at the same time the narrator gently urges us to recognise the essentially shallow nature of the heroine'.[5] Its function is certainly ironic but, it seems to me, the irony works the other way: to suggest the essentially shallow nature of Niel.

*A Lost Lady* has been called a Middle Western *Madame Bovary*; a tale of adultery in a provincial, bourgeois setting. Indeed, writers dealing with this theme after Flaubert could hardly fail to echo *Madame Bovary* – and Cather is no exception.[6] For example, when Marian hears that her lover, Frank Ellinger, is to be married she becomes desperate and tries to telephone him on his wedding night even though by doing so she risks exposure. In the description of her 'blue lips' and 'the black shadows under her eyes' which 'made her look as if some poison were at work in her body' (131) it is imposible not to think of her French prototype. There are certain superficial similarities of plot: both women live in a backwater and pine for the high life, take lovers, drink too much and end up in debt. But the differences are equally obvious: Marian's debts are honourable ones (and not of her making); Captain Forrester is nothing like Charles Bovary and Marian's life does not end in tragedy. Most important of all is the difference in attitude towards the heroine: Flaubert may have said 'Madame Bovary, c'est moi' but he also said that in writing about her he sometimes had 'a physical desire to vomit'; Cather said Marian Forrester was based on a woman she had known in her youth whose 'lovely hair and laughter made [her] happy clear down to [her] toes'.[7]

Cather also said that she wanted to portray Marian's 'effect' on Niel and in so doing he becomes as important as the lady herself. In the creation of his character, for which there is no parallel in *Madame Bovary*, Cather's novel comes much closer to *L'Éducation Sentimentale*. In her essay 'A Chance Meeting', there is a lengthy discussion of Flaubert and her account of meeting his niece, Madame Grout, reveals just how much his work, which Cather had been reading since childhood, meant to her: 'It was like being brought up against a mountain of memories. One could not see round it; one could only stupidly realize that in this mountain . . . lay most of one's mental past.' What she admired in Flaubert are the things he 'stood for . . . that peculiar integrity of language and vision, that coldness which, in him, is somehow noble'. *Madame Bovary* she refuses to discuss: 'it is a fact in history. One knows it too well to know it well.' But *L'Éducation Sentimentale* she thinks underrated:

It had seemed to me . . . that its very faults were of a noble kind. It is too cold, certainly, to justify the subtitle, 'Roman d'un jeune homme'; for youth, even when it has not generous enthusiasm, has at least fierce egotism. But I had wondered whether this cool, dispassionate, almost contemptuous presentation of Frédéric were not a protest against the overly sympathetic manner of Balzac in his stories of young men . . .[8]

*A Lost Lady* is in sharp contrast to any of Cather's earlier novels. Jim Burden, although not 'overly' so, is a sympathetic narrator and Cather herself, like Balzac with his heroes, had got 'into the ring' and sweated a little on behalf of Thea Kronburg. But here, the narrative voice is like Flaubert's: cool, dispassionate, like 'dry wine'. Only once does the narrator directly express any concern for the heroine; in the first, expositional chapter where the Forrester's house is described: 'He grew old there – and even she, alas! grew older' (8). After that one interjection the tone throughout remains impersonal; at no point does the narrator intervene directly to guide the reader's response.

Something of Cather's intention in portraying a young man's obsession with an older woman is revealed through her assessment in 'A Chance Meeting' of Flaubert's limitations:

Of course, a story of youth which altogether leaves out that gustatory zest, that exaggerated concern for trivialities, is scarcely successful. In *L'Éducation* the trivialities are there (for life is made up of them), but not the voracious appetite which drives young people through silly and vulgar experiences. The story of Frédéric is the story of youth with the heart left out . . .

By incorporating so many of Niel's thoughts and feelings, Cather's is a story of youth with the heart left in. There is a 'glow' and 'ardour' in the novel, emanating from Marian Forrester, and transmitted to us through the generous, egotistical, silly, young Niel.

One of the most crucial episodes in Niel's sentimental education shows both Flaubert's influence and the operation of irony. One morning, when the Captain is away, Niel sets off to pay a call on Mrs Forrester and is shattered to discover that she has a lover. The reader, however, already knows this for we have seen Marian and Frank Ellinger through Adolph Blum's eyes. Cather deliberately forestalls any possibility of suspense, so that during the whole of Niel's walk to the Forrester place we are aware of how completely he has misjudged the situation. The flowers he gathers for her patently will not produce the effect he desires: 'When she opened her shutters to let in the light, she would find them, – and they would perhaps give her a sudden distaste for coarse worldlings like Frank Ellinger' (83). Almost immediately, he becomes aware that Frank is in the bedroom with her.

Niel derives a bitter satisfaction in finding the perfect expression for his disgust at her deception: '"Lilies that fester," he muttered, *"lilies that fester smell far worse than weeds"*' (84). Although the narrator makes no comment, there has been a careful preparation for this scene. Immediately before it the reader learns that Niel is an avid reader of the Romantics; Byron's *Don Juan* and Goethe's *Wilhelm Meister*. The other side of his character is drawn to the scepticism and restraint of Montaigne but it is Ovid's *Heroides* which most fully captures his imagination. These epistles of unhappy and abandoned women, whose sufferings are rendered with equal sympathy whether they are virtuous, adulterous, or even incestuous, echo throughout the novel – most particularly in the frantic letters sent by Marian to Ellinger. To Niel, the *Heroides* 'were the most glowing love stories ever told' (78). He finds in the philandering male persona of *Don Juan* a little '"fooling"' but none at all in the amours of the women: 'He was eavesdropping upon the past, being let into the great world that had plunged and glittered and sumptuously sinned long before little Western towns were ever dreamed of' (79).

When he makes his way to Mrs Forrester he is full of romantic idealism and he thinks of his bunch of

flowers as a 'bouquet for a lovely lady' (82). He places
her on a pedestal and is wholly ignorant of the reality
of her life. When he is forced to recognise that she
is not a beautiful object but a passionate woman, he
is disgusted: 'Beautiful women . . . was their brilliancy
always fed by something coarse and concealed? Was that
their secret?' (84). Ironically, the very qualities which he
relishes in literature are abhorrent to him in reality. He
turns away and throws his flowers in the mud: 'In that
instant between stooping to the window-sill and rising, he
had lost one of the most beautiful things in his life' (83).

   *L'Éducation Sentimentale* provides an interesting perspective on the nature of this loss. Although Cather finds
fault with aspects of the novel she has only praise for its
'great and quiet last scene': 'One is "left with it," in the
sane way that one is left with a weak heart after certain
illnesses. A shadow has come into one's consciousness that
will not go out again.' The 'shadow' referred to here is like
the 'chilling doubt' (97) which the morning call on Mrs
Forrester instils in Niel. The final scene in *L'Éducation*
portrays Frédéric and Deslauriers remembering their visit
to the Turkish woman's brothel. The two boys had arrived
holding nosegays for the lovely ladies but at the last
moment, filled with terror and embarassment, they had
thrown their flowers in the mud and fled:

> 'That was the happiest time we ever had,' said Frédéric.
> 'Yes, perhaps you're right. That was the happiest time
> we ever had,' said Deslauriers.[9]

Their nostalgia is not for a lost innocence. They treasure
that moment of turning back, not because they had retained
their purity, but because they still had their illusions. In
the same way, Cather's *jeune hommet* does not suffer from
the 'outrage' to a 'moral scruple' but to an 'aesthetic ideal'

(84). It is in this sense that Mrs Forrester is a lost lady; less a symbol of a lost pioneer age than of Niel's lost illusions.

Niel's reflections during his walk to Mrs Forrester's house reveal that his rejection of her is based on his inability to acknowledge his own sexuality. He sets off early imagining that 'he would get over to the hill before Frank Ellinger could intrude his unwelcome presence' (81). He feels that there is 'an almost religious purity about the fresh morning air' and as he wonders 'why he did not often come over like this, to see the day before men and their activities had spoiled it, while the morning was still unsullied' (82), one can see him attempting to transform Sweet Water into the Garden of Eden. His distaste particularly for 'men's activities', is a refusal of manhood and his emphasis on the morning's purity represents his longing to inhabit a world before the Fall and the 'intrusion' of sex.

This fear of sexuality translates itself into a neurotic desire for stasis; an inability to either grow up himself or accept change of any kind. When he returns home from college two years later he finds that the Forresters have come down in the world and that they are now dependent on Ivy Peters, who had once belonged to the very lowest echelons of Sweet Water's social hierarchy. Niel is saddened that the Captain has been forced to lease his meadowland to the town's 'shyster lawyer' to grow wheat:

The Old West had been settled by dreamers, great-hearted adventurers who were unpractical to the point of magnificence; a courteous brotherhood, strong in attack but weak in defence, who could conquer but could not hold. Now all the vast territory they had won was to be at the mercy of men like Ivy Peters, who had never dared anything, never risked anything. They would drink up the mirage, dispel the morning freshness, root out the great brooding spirit of freedom, the generous, easy life of the great land-holders. The

space, the colour, the princely carelessness of the pioneer
they would destroy and cut up into profitable bits, as the
match factory splinters the primeval forest. All the way
from the Missouri to the mountains this generation of
shrewd young men, trained to petty economies by hard
times, would do exactly what Ivy Peters had done when
he drained the Forrester marsh. (104–105)

This passage is invariably cited by critics as Cather's
nostalgic lament for the passing of the pioneer age, despite
the fact that she clearly distances herself from it by stating
at the outset, 'Niel played with his idea'. The most
striking aspect of Niel's account is the way in which
the pioneers are designated by adjectives and the men
like Ivy Peters in terms of verbs. The pioneers were
'great-hearted', 'courteous', 'unpractical', 'careless', 'easy'
and 'generous'. The only verbs employed in association
with them are the conditional ('could conquer'), the negative
('could not hold') and, significantly, 'settled'. Although
the usurpers had 'never dared', 'never risked', as the
pioneers had once done, only they display any energy
now: they 'drink up', 'dispel', 'root out', 'destroy' and
'cut up'. To Niel, their activity is wholly destructive.
His refusal to accept change is linked to his rejection of
sexuality: the phrase 'dispel the morning freshness' recalls
his disillusioning expedition to Mrs Forrester's bedroom.

Niel's mythologising of the pioneers as 'dreamers' and
'princes' is not without value and neither is his idolisation
of Mrs Forrester. His perceptions are distorted only when
he will not allow that there is any value in the present or
in Mrs Forrester once she ceases to conform to his ideal.
When the Captain dies she is left friendless and poor. Ivy
Peters improves her finances but she has to pay for this
by becoming his lover. Although none of the Captain's old
friends helps her, and Niel actively dissaudes them from
doing so, he is outraged at her attempts to save herself:

It was what he most held against Mrs Forrester; that she was not willing to immolate herself, like the widow of all these great men, and die with the pioneer period to which she belonged; that she preferred life on any terms. In the end, Niel went away without bidding her goodbye. He went away with weary contempt for her in his heart. (172)

Again, it is not, as is so often stated, Cather who is speaking here: it does not show her disgust with life, but Niel's.[10] The final comment on the limitations of his perspective is made obliquely at the end of the novel. After many years he hears that Mrs Forrester had remarried and lives in Argentina. Ed Elliot, who had seen her there, tells Niel that she was well and happy and sent Niel her love. In the two men's final exchange Cather makes us feel, not only Elliot's good nature, but his relief that Niel is not going to be contemptuous and grudging:

'So we may feel that she was well cared for, to the very end,' said Niel. 'Thank God for that!'
'I knew you'd feel that way,' said Ed Elliot, as a warm wave of feeling passed over his face. 'I did!' (177–178)

Ed Elliot is one of the 'new breed' of men coming out of the West that Niel had despised. Born the son of the town cobbler, he is now a prosperous mining engineer: 'a broad-shouldered man with an open, sunbrowned face' (175); frank and generous. By giving him the last word in the novel, Cather holds out some hope for the future: there is an alternative to the noble old Captain whose day is done and the cynical and corrupt Ivy Peters whom Niel fears is taking over.

Cather wrote in a letter that the novel's integrity depended on the Captain and our conception of him is dominated by the image of an old man seated in front of a sun-dial, stoically watching '"time visibly devoured"' (110).[11] In every aspect of his life he is dignified, courageous and honest: when the bank, to which he had lent his name, fails he pays the depositors out of his own money; he delights in his wife's charm and beauty and, though he knows very well that she has a lover, he adores and protects her. He is not 'time's fool'. Although Niel admires the Captain he is nothing like him. The Captain is loyal to the things and people he 'values'; Niel, in the name of loyalty, betrays them. And the Captain's fidelity is returned: even though Marian is technically "unfaithful" she never complains of poverty, she nurses him through his illness and after his death sends flowers to his grave each year.

And what of Marian Forrester herself? Cather stated that she had not attempted a character study but a portrait.[12] She is seen from various perspectives but never from within; in the end she remains ambiguous. The reader witnesses her 'effect' – on the boys of the town, the Captain's friends and on Niel, who all succumb to her charm. Cather tells very little about her past; there are only scattered references to the 'stories' circulated about the 'gay life' (74) she led in Colorado and to how she came to marry the Captain. Marian's own account of how she had slipped on a mountain-climbing expedition and he had carried her, is a metaphor of their marriage: '"I knew . . . he would never drop me"' (168). He is the ony one who does not; Niel's priggish idealism, Ellinger's sensual indulgence and Ivy's passionless embrace, all fail her.

After the Captain's stroke, Mrs Forrester is confined to Sweet Water and deprived of society. On Niel's return home from college she relates how she had visited friends at Glenwood Springs:

'I always know how I am looking, and I looked well enough. The men thought so. I looked happier than any

woman there . . . I accepted the Dalzell's invitation with
a purpose; I wanted to see whether I had anything left
worth saving. And I have, I tell you!' (125)

Like Madame Bovary, she '"plans"' and '"plots"'
how to '"get out of this hole"' (125) and return to
the scene of excitement: '"Perhaps people think that
I've settled down to grow old gracefully, but I've not.
I feel such a power to live in me"' (124). But without
men to admire her and women to compete with, she barely
exists. After her husband's death, preferring 'life on any
terms' (172) – and life for her, as for Emma Bovary, means
having a lover – she becomes Ivy's mistress.

Cather's essay 'The Novel Démeublé provides a key to
the lost lady. In it she rejects Naturalism as a dehumanising
catalogue and advocates an art of selection. She wanted
to free fiction from the accretion of fact which had
clung to it like a dead weight:

> How wonderful it would be if we could throw all the
> furniture out of the window and, along with it, all the
> meaningless reiterations concerning physical sensations,
> all the tiresome old patterns . . . leave the scene bare for
> the play of emotions, great and little – [13]

She was not interested in the novel as a social document and
she felt that novelists too often regarded form as a matter
of taking one of the stock moulds off the shelf, instead of
finding or creating, the form which suited the material.

Her prescription for the novel is really a description
of what she herself had done in A Lost Lady. She asks
if the story of a banker's marital and financial difficulties
is 'at all reinforced by a masterly exposition of banking,
our whole system of credits, the methods of the Stock
Exchange?' Balzac and Zola certainly thought it was but

Cather deals with the bank failure in a couple of pages; she was not concerned with the system itself, only its effect on people's lives. In *A Lost Lady* she sketches the social map of Sweet Water in a few bold strokes; 'that drudge, the theme writing high-school student, sent there for information regarding the manners and dress and interiors' of the period would not find out very much.

It is not that Cather disliked description but it had to serve a greater purpose than the gratification of the interior designer. She cites Tolstoy, 'almost as great a lover of material things as Balzac':

> But there is this determining difference: the clothes, the dishes, the haunting interiors of those old Moscow houses are always so much part of the people that they are perfectly synthesized; they seem to exist not so much in the author's mind as in the emotional penumbra of the characters themselves.

This is a perfect analysis of her own treatment of interiors in *A Lost Lady*, for the house is inextricably linked in Niel's mind with the total effect produced by Mrs Forrester. The novel never leaves the Forrester place; at first it is the gracious setting in which Marian exercises her charm and later it becomes a dark hole from which she has to claw her way out.

The essay sets up an opposition between 'literalness' and the power of 'suggestion':

> Whatever is felt upon the page without being specifically named there – that, one might say, is created. It is the inexplicable presence of the thing not named, of the overtone divined by the ear but not heard by it, the verbal mood, the emotional aura of the fact or the thing or the deed, that gives high quality to the novel or the drama, as well as to poetry itself.

And in a letter to F. Scott Fitzgerald Cather said that
*A Lost Lady* was about personal charm and the enigma
of beauty; of how much greater the effect is than its
cause.[14] The novel is built on the discrepancy between
empirical fact and poetic truth. The Forrester place, for
example, 'was not at all remarkable'; 'stripped of its vines
. . . [it] would probably have been ugly enough' (4–5). It
is only made to seem beautiful by the people who live in
it. When Mrs Forrester is ill the townswomen invade the
house where formerly 'they had never got past the parlour',
and which had always seemed so alluring, only to find
'they had been fooled all these years . . . The kitchen
was inconvenient, the sink was smelly' (138). But these
facts, which they pounce on as 'reality', cannot take away
from the 'aura' that the house had always had.

In the same way Niel feels he has been fooled by
Mrs Forrester: she is not what she had seemed; she
drinks too much and takes lovers. And yet the memory
of her haunts him:

> Her eyes, when they laughed for a moment into one's
> own, seemed to promise a wild delight that he had not
> found in life. 'I know where it is,' they seemed to say,
> 'I could show you!' He would like to call up the shade
> of the young Mrs Forrester . . . and challenge it, demand
> the secret of that ardour; ask her whether she had really
> found some ever-blooming, ever-burning, ever-piercing
> joy, or whether it was all fine play-acting. Probably
> she had found no more than another; but she had
> always the power of suggesting things much lovelier
> than herself, as the perfume of a single flower may
> call up the whole sweetness of spring. (174–175)

Niel's vision, here, is still restricted; he suspects it was
all play-acting, that Marian had not *really* found more in
life than anyone else. And he is still unable to accept

change: the joy must be 'ever-blooming', 'ever-burning', in order to satisfy him. But even if he could challenge her, he would not get at the 'truth' because, Cather implies, the truth is not made up of unalterable facts that can be known and classified and made to stand still. Although it is lost to Niel, Cather celebrates the gift of poetry, the power of suggestion, in the character of Marian Forrester and in the novel as a whole. Whatever the facts of Mrs Forrester's life, her evocation of loveliness is the most meaningful thing in Niel's.

It is a chastening irony that *A Lost Lady* should have been seen by so many critics as a life-denying essay in bitterness. It offers instead a sometimes sad exploration of time and change and memory but always at the core there is a 'promise' of 'delight' for those who will accept it. There is no call for Niel's resentment and disillusion; as Eudora Welty said, 'what a lesson *A Lost Lady* gives us in doing without bitterness.'[15] It is a lesson which Cather's Professor also has to learn.

# 6  To speak of the woe that is in marriage:

## The Professors's House

Que sert à vos pareils de lire incessamment
Ils sont toujours logés à la troisieme chambre.

La Fontaine[1]

Flounder, flounder, in the sea,
Come, I pray thee, here to me;
For my wife, good Ilsabil,
Wills not as I'd have her will.

Virginia Woolf, *To The Lighthouse*[2]

*The Professor's House* is a very strange book for a woman
to have written; not because the central character is a man
but because he is a man besieged by difficult women. The
Professor suffers because he is alive, because he has reached
the time of life when death becomes a reality, casting an
ironic perspective on all that has gone before; but beyond
this existential pain he suffers particularly, as a man. The
underlying theme of the novel is the relation between the
sexes and its collapse: by the end of the novel the Professor
has been completely estranged from his wife and daughters,

having been rejected, humiliated and disappointed by each of them in turn. Conventionally, the subject is part of male territory; indeed, it has become something of an American male speciality. The middle-aged man, driven to manic distraction or lonely despair by the modern world, and particularly the women in it, is a major theme for writers otherwise as diverse as Ernest Hemingway, Saul Bellow and Norman Mailer. It is the fictional equivalent of the bar-room drunk crying that his wife doesn't understand him and is as tedious as it is ubiquitous. It will not, I hope, be necessary to go on a pub crawl to appreciate that Cather's treatment of this theme is rather different.

Male critics have often been disgruntled at Cather's presumption in employing male narrators and protaganists, notwithstanding that she did so convincingly. Feminist critics have tended to ignore *The Professor's House* in order to concentrate on her compelling female characters – Alexandra, Thea, Ántonia – on the assumption that in a literature dominated by men, female characters have been defined in masculine terms and that the most radical and interesting contribution women writers have made is in portraying them in their own. Cather herself had little interest in feminism.[3] Like so many successful women of her time, she recognised the obstacles but thought that the strong woman would simply override them. Unlike Virgina Woolf she was not a dedicated reader of women's writing; she displayed a bland indifference to the question of women's position in society and her aesthetic theory was not informed by any consideration of sexual difference. Her exploration of male characters is completely uninhibited and her treatment of the interaction of men and women is without specific feminist intention.

*The Professor's House* does not directly present any scenes between the mother and daughters in which the Professor is absent but, although attention is always focused on him, the women are allowed their say and the reader is aware of their independent life; their preoccupations, desires and disappointments. A lesser writer, particularly perhaps if he were male, would have minimised the validity of the wife's complaints against her husband; a tendency which I hope to illustrate later by a comparison with Anatole France's *The Wicker Work Woman*. Godfrey St Peter is hurt by his wife but Cather does not try to gain sympathy for him at Lillian's expense. When Lillian accuses him of growing '"more intolerant all the time"' and Cather tells us that 'the thing that stuck in his mind constantly was that she was growing more and more intolerant' (35), they both express the truth as they perceive it.

Unhappy marriages abound in literature and they are each, to paraphrase Tolstoy, unhappy in their own way. Moreover, in writing about this, men and women have not necessarily sided with their own sex – far from it. What is rare is Cather's complete absence of partisanship; her ability to suspend judgement. As she wrote in *My Mortal Enemy* (1926) – another story of marital breakdown: '"A man and a woman draw apart from that long embrace, and see *what they have done to each other*."'[4] (Emphasis added.)

It is also rare to find a woman novelist capable of portraying such a thoroughly convincing and sympathetic male character. Virginia Woolf identified physical description as the first hurdle:

> . . . no one will admit that he can possibly mistake a novel written by a man for a novel written by a woman . . . . Each sex describes itself. The first words in which either a man or a woman is described are generally enough to determine the sex of the writer.[5]

It would, I think, be impossible to determine the author's sex at any point in the novel and certainly not from St Peter's first appearance: 'The Professor in pyjamas was not an unpleasant sight; for looks, the fewer clothes he had on

the better. Anything that clung to his body showed it to be
built upon extremely good bones, with the slender hips and
springy shoulders of a tireless swimmer' (12). Here there
is neither prudery and embarassment, nor bragging; the
Professor can be contained within his swimming trunks.

*The Professor's House* is usually interpreted as a
polemic against commercial values, mass production
and the misuse of science; a product of Cather's
'disgust' with contemporary life.[6] But the social and
historical concerns which have preoccupied critics do
not constitute the most interesting aspect of the novel
and my discussion of them will remain peripheral to the
main theme of the relations between the sexes.

The novel begins after the St Peters have moved into
their new house; built with the prize money from the
Professor's *Spanish Adventurers in North America*. The old
house is cold, inconvenient and shabby but it is the place
where the children were born and where the Professor had
done his most important work. He is reluctant to move
and continues to rent the old house in order to use his
attic study. His wife cannot understand this. Critics too
have been baffled and have sought explanations in Cather's
own life.[7] In 1916 Isabelle McClung married the violinist, Jan
Hambourg, to whom the novel is dedicated and on whom
Louie Marsellus is said to be based. Cather was devastated
by Isabelle's marriage and although they remained friends
– Cather even came to like Jan Hambourg – it was one of
the most traumatic events in her life. She not only lost
her friend's exclusive affection, but the attic sewing room
in Isabelle's house where she had worked for over fifteen
years. The Hambourgs wanted to build a study for her
in their marital home but Cather refused as she felt she
could not work there, just as the Professor declines the
offer of a study in the Marsellus's new house.

Leon Edel suggests that the relationship between the
two women was either 'actively or latently lesbian'; that

Cather regarded Isabelle's marriage as an act of betrayal and her anger and grief found their way into *The Professor's House*. This 'explains' the otherwise inexplicable depression of Professor St Peter. Edel states that 'Cather is so identified with her professor that she is unable to supply a "rejection motif" for his despair. All she could say was that the world was out of joint for him – as it was for her.' Because of this Edel finds the book flawed and 'unrealised'. However, his contention that the biographer can date a change in her novels from the year of Isabelle's marriage (1916) is not strictly accurate. Her 'increasing tension and deep uneasiness' may be reflected in *One of Ours* (1922), *A Lost Lady* (1923) and the novel in question, but *My Ántonia* – published in 1918 – is certainly not an 'anxious book' nor imbued with a sense of betrayal.

Fascinating as such biographical speculation may be, it must be remembered that Cather wrote *The Professor's House* eight years after Isabelle's marriage from a perspective, one hopes, of emotion recollected in some tranquillity. Moreover, as I hope to show, the Professor is given a credible motivation and psychology, independent of his creator, and the novel can stand on its own without recourse to external exegesis.

Godfrey claims that it is only in his old study that he can work; he clings to it out of habit, but part of his unhappiness is due to the fact that the *Spanish Adventurers* is finished and he has nothing to take its place. The old house too is where the St Peters had lived as a family, the new one is to be occupied only by him and Lillian. In Chapter II Mrs St Peter, who had directed the building and all the arrangements, tries to persuade Godfrey of the merits of their new home: '"And it's much more dignified, at your age, to have a room of your own."' An assertion of that kind is hard to answer and one can detect an understandable defensiveness in his reply: '"It's convenient, certainly, though I hope I'm not so old as to be personally repulsive?"' (34). In the course of the novel it is revealed that the Professor is fifty-two!

Chapter III opens, after the first night in separate rooms, with the Professor wishing that 'he could be transported on his mattress from the new house to the old': 'But it was Sunday, and on that day his wife always breakfasted with him. There was no way out; they would meet at compt' (46). As the barbed comments fly across the coffee percolator the reader learns that Godfrey is disappointed that his daughter had married the florid, voluble, Louie Marsellus and is surprised that Lillian should accept him into the family so warmly. Rosamund had once been engaged to his favourite pupil, Tom Outland, who had been killed in the war, and as a result the Professor has '"no enthusiasm"' for being a father-in-law. He admits that only Lillian '"keep[s] the ball rolling"' (49). The scene establishes her position: she holds the family together and is right about Marsellus.

Once the conversation ends, we learn more about the tensions in the marriage from the Professor's viewpoint:

> As he left the house, he was reflecting that people who are intensely in love when they marry, and who go on being in love, always meet with something which suddenly or gradually makes a difference. Sometimes it is the children, or the grubbiness of being poor, sometimes a second infatuation. In their own case it had been, curiously enough, his pupil, Tom Outland. (49)

The passage is striking in its finality, in the assumption that something 'always' makes a difference, and its almost Olympian detachment: 'curiously enough', he reflects, as if he were observing the domestic habits of penguins. He is without rancour; almost, it seems, without regret.

The pain of being rejected sexually is alluded to again when the projected trip to Paris is discussed. The Professor will not go, less because of Louie whom he now likes, than because of Lillian and Rosamund whom he feels have 'changed bewilderingly . . . and hardened' (161). The Professor withdraws more and more from family life; once he ceases to be Lillian's lover he feels redundant:

> Besides, he would not be needed. He could trust Louie to take care of Lillian, and nobody could please her more than her son-in-law. *Beaux-fils*, apparently, were meant by Providence to take the husband's place when husbands had ceased to be lovers. (160)

While most people would consider being in love with someone as the most intimate of all relations, for the Professor it creates primarily a social bond, with the original impulse of the lover being rapidly smothered and distorted by social obligations. During the summer of his family's absence he reflects that:

> The man he was now, the personality his friends knew, had begun to grow strong during adolescence, during the years when he was always consciously or unconsciously conjugating the verb 'to love' . . . . When he met Lillian, it reached its maturity . . . . One thing led to another . . . and the design of his life had been the work of this secondary social man, the lover . . . . Because there was Lillian, there must be marriage and a salary. Because there was marriage, there were children . . . (264–265)

This is a very sympathetic account of the 'trap' of marriage and very different from the cynical cliché, perpetrated by a certain kind of male literature, of the man being harnessed by the woman and flogged to death in support of her and the children. Groping for the moment when things had gone wrong, he blames the lover but much of the problem is the 'social man'; the conditions imposed on the lover by the society in which he lives.

To St Peter this social man is secondary to the pre-adolescent Kansas boy who constitutes his 'original, unmodified' self (263) – unmodified, that is, by sex. In middle-age this boy returns to him, bringing a new, disquieting awareness that 'his career, his wife, his family, were not his life at all, but a chain of events which happened to him' (264). In his alienation from this secondary social man he discovers that he is alone, that he has always been so, and that the feeling he had between boyhood and middle age that he was not, was an illusion: 'He seemed to know, among other things, that he was solitary and must always be so . . . . He was earth and would return to earth'. He is separated not only from his family but from his work: he 'was not a scholar' and 'his histories . . . had no more to do with his original ego than his daughters had'. Books and children 'were a result of the high pressure of young manhood' (265). The image of the successful man with a big career, a beautiful wife and children becomes no more to him than an expression of libido and egocentricity. The cornerstone of his adult life is his relation with Lillian and when that is dislodged the whole edifice topples. As the summer comes to an end and his wife's return is imminent, he is thrown into a panic: 'There must, he was repeating to himself, there must be some way in which a man who had always tried to live up to his repsonsibilities could, when the hour of desperation came, avoid meeting his own familiy' (274).

He becomes terrified of human contact. Through the force of habit and obligation, the Professor had only been dimly aware that something was wrong but in the summer vacation, with his family away, the machinery of his life grinds to a halt. He does not know where he had 'made his mistake' (275) but he knows that one has been made. He tells himself: '"Surely the saddest thing is falling out of love – if once one has ever fallen in"' (275). It leaves him completely alienated. The vision which informs the novel is profoundly pessimistic; based on an awareness of the irreconcilable elements in the human condition:

> One realises that human relationships are the tragic necessity of human life; that they can never be wholly satisfactory, that every ego is half the time greedily seeking them, and half the time pulling away from them.[8]

By the end of the novel the Professor is no longer struggling to achieve or to possess: he does not regret his past life but he is indifferent to it. Weary of the cycle of desire and disappointment, he drifts towards renunciation. When the 'long-anticipated coincidence' happens (276) - the storm blows the windows shut and the stove out – he surrenders to fate. He is saved by Augusta but, after his temporary release from consciousness, he is not the same man: 'He had let something go – and it was gone: something very precious, that he could not consciously have relinquished, probably' (282). Although he is not aware of having done so he had apparently tried to save himself. The accident represents, not the denial of the will to live, but the abnegation of desire. In an attempt to escape from the tragic necessity of human relations he renounces all forms of passion.

St Peter's sense of isolation, of how arbitrary his life has been, is precipitated by an awareness of death but after the accident he is not simply waiting to die. And he is no longer cowering at the prospect of his wife's return: 'He thought he knew where he was, and that he could face with fortitude the *Berengaria* and the future' (283). The novel ends with these lines and with the suggestion that, though his life has changed, it is not over. But if the human lot is to desire, what future can there be for one who has surrendered that possibility? St Peter stands at the edge of a new frontier: he has gone beyond love, a career, a family, into a new territory beyond desire. One journey is over but a new one is beginning: 'There was still Augusta, however; a world full of Augustas, with whom one was *outward bound*' (281, emphasis added).

Augusta is the devout German Catholic woman who comes to sew for the family twice a year and with whom the Professor had shared his 'cuddy'. She is humorous, pious and utterly without pretension. In the first part of the novel the Professor patronises her but in the final part his attitude changes:

> She wasn't at all afraid to say things that were heavily, drearily true, and though he used to wince under them, he hurried off with the feeling that they were good for him . . . . Augusta was like the taste of bitter herbs; she was the bloomless side of life that he had always run away from, – yet when he had to face it, he found that it wasn't altogether repugnant. (280)

She becomes a kind of flat-footed personification of wisdom. He recalls how she had often been 'needed' when there had been a death in one of the families for whom she sewed but that she had none of 'the equivocal American way of dealing with serious facts' (272) that the Professor notes in the sham upholstery put in coffins. She faces reality squarely: 'She talked about death as she spoke of a hard winter or a rainy March, or any of the other sadnesses of nature' (281).

The Professor loses touch with his family; the vital interest he had felt in all their concerns evaporates. They sail back to America, because Rosamund is to have a baby, at the time when he has come close to death. They are at the top of the wheel of life at the time when he feels he has fallen off it. Hardly overjoyed at the prospect of becoming a grandfather, he finds that he would rather be with Augusta. By her presence, her 'image', he reorientates his life but this is not to say that he embraces Catholicism or that Cather was advocating renunciation as a mode of living. She gave a copy of the novel to Robert Frost inscribed, 'This is really a story of "letting go with the heart" but most reviewers seem to consider it an attempt to popularize a system of philosophy.'[9]

The implications of Augusta's single state are quite as important as her Catholicism. The major difference between her and the other women in the novel is that she is not defined by her sex. Cather says nothing of her social relations except that she is [Appelhof's] 'niece and a spinster' (10). She arrives to sew and leaves to sew at other people's houses. Nothing in the descriptions of Augusta emphasises the fact that she is a woman: 'She herself was tall, large-boned, flat and stiff, with a plain, solid face, and brown eyes not destitute of fun' (23). She has large hands and a fine head of hair. Unlike so many spinsters in literature she is not ridiculous, pitiable or grotesque. Her life is not dependent on love, marriage or children. When the Professor lets go with the heart he loses his sexual identity and is outward bound with Augusta.

In contrast to her, Lillian, Rosamund and Kitty always appear in the context of the home. All are married, none of them works and, although Kitty and her mother both studied at University, they have never considered the possibility of a career. Superficially, Lillian appears almost a copybook stereotype of the 'feminine' woman: beautiful, cruel, indulgent, exacting, charming, scheming and worldly. Most 'feminine' of all, she is intuitive and irrational: 'With her really radiant charm, she had a very interesting mind – but it was quite wrong to call it mind . . . What she had was a richly endowed nature' (49–50). At first sight it looks as if Cather is perpetuating all the old myths. Lillian, though forceful and intelligent, lives vicariously – she is the woman behind every great man:

Yes, with her sons-in-law she had begun the game of being a woman all over again. She dressed for them, planned for them, schemed in their interests

. . . . [She] lived in their careers as she had once done in his. It was splendid, St Peter told himself. She wasn't going to have to face a stretch of boredom between being a young woman and being a young grandmother. (79)

But these are the Professor's thoughts. What he 'told himself' is extremely patronising, with Lillian's sphere of influence belittlingly designated as 'the little anxious social world of Hamilton'. According to the Professor her life is biologically determined: she has children, then grandchildren and in the little lull in between she is to charm and scheme (having only had daughters) for her sons-in-law. Because she is a woman he evisages her life, not as a course of action, but as a state or condition: 'being' a young woman and 'being' a grandmother. The Professor has the serious activity known as work, she 'the game of being a woman'.

There is a moment in the novel when it is intimated that Lillian does not find all this scheming and charming as fulfilling as he imagines:

'My dear,' he sighed . . . 'it's been a mistake, our having a family and writing histories and getting middle-aged. We should have been picturesquely shipwrecked together when we were young.'
'How often I've thought that!' she replied with a faint, melancholy smile.
'You? . . . ' he murmured in astonishment. (94)

He 'wished he knew just how it seemed to her' (95) but it has apparently never occurred to him to ask. For Lillian it is too late: 'There was something lonely and forgiving in her voice, something that spoke of an old wound, healed and hardened and hopeless' (94). Although Lillian is invariably portrayed from the Professor's point of view there is an unstated perspective. His descriptions of family life are so completely self-orientated that the reader is bound to wonder 'how it seemed to her'. Cather's emphasis on his 'amazement' at not understanding his wife alerts the reader to the limitation of his perceptions.

Shortly after this episode he indulges in this astonishingly complacent reflection:

> All the while he had been working so fiercely at his eight big volumes, he was not insensible to the domestic drama that went on beneath him . . . . Just as, when Queen Mathilde was doing the long tapestry now shown at Bayeux, – working her chronicle of the deeds of Knights and heroes, – alongside the big pattern of dramatic action she and her women carried the little playful pattern of birds and beasts that are a story in themselves; so, to him, the most important chapters of his history were interwoven with personal memories. (101)

Perhaps he dedicated each of his eight big volumes, 'To my wife, without whom . . . '! The novel offers a classic portrait of the writer and the writer's wife: exactly the scenario which historically made it so much easier for men to work than women; the presence of what Virgina Woolf termed the 'Angel in the House', who cooks, cleans, cares for the children and even dispenses flowers and charming conversation when the man descends from his labours.

I am conscious of the possibility of attributing to Cather a 'feminist' awareness that she may not have possessed. Cather considered that the artist had special needs and she may have regarded a privileged position as his prerogative. However, she states in a letter that Virgina Woolf gives a fair account of the problems of being a woman writer and she may also have agreed with Woolf that this was neither a necessary nor natural state of affairs.[10] It is not, then, implausible to see this passage as a veiled criticism of the marital status quo and to see it as being deliberately, if obliquely, intended to function as such.

This reading would seem to be supported by the Professor's comparison with the Bayeux tapestry. A.S. Byatt comments on it in her introduction to the Virago edition: 'St Peter compares the household work of his womenfolk whilst he was writing, to the women who embroidered birds and beasts in the Bayeux tapestry whilst history unfolded.' This is no doubt what he intends: he is engaged on 'the big pattern of dramatic action' while his wife and daughters carry 'the little playful pattern alongside'. But his easy classification of importance – big and little – fails to convince. Moreover, despite its logical framework ('just as', 'so') the comparison is confused, for the Queen and her women work *all* the tapestry, big and little. The Professor wants to hog the centre for himself and his History and to push the women to the sidelines but the allusion to the Bayeux tapestry, in fact, works against him. That this interpretatio should be possible is not the result of negligence on Cather's part, or an imposition of meaning on my own. By inserting the phrase, 'so, to him', she carefully distances herself from his specious reasoning and exposes his masculine bias.

It is not always easy to 'place' the Professor or to decide how far his viewpoint is endorsed and how much is ironic and questionable. Among critics he has had both partisans and detractors but in the end this is beside the point. Cather identified with him and borrowed many of her own experiences and beliefs for the creation of his character. In his compassion, humour and integrity it is not difficult for most readers to sympathise with him. None the less his perceptions are distorted, and distorted specifically, by his masculinity. Cather presents his thoughts without comment but this does not mean that they are hers. She refuses to make judgements and merely sets before the reader a complex psychology and interaction of characters. The Bayeux tapestry, for example, is one of several images through which Cather subtly, almost slyly, tests and explores the way men and women respond to each other and the limitations of strict masculine and feminine roles.

The Professor's masculine viewpoint is also evident in his attitude to Rosamund and Kitty. They are both defined by him as women and particularly as wives. He considers that Kathleen would have been happier if she had made a better marriage but it never occurs to him that she should not depend on a man, regretting only that she chose one with 'a usual sort of mind' (66). Although she is a talented painter, instead of encouraging her, he congratulates her on her lack of ambition. Kitty thinks she is ordinary, unlike the girls in the Professor's class who, if they '"have a spark of aptitude for anything seem to think themselves remarkable"' (65). One wonders if he adopts the same positive attitude with the boys! Kathleen's independence and wilfulness disturb St Peter; he wants to 'make her take his arm and be docile' (64). Later, he is disappointed that she grows frustrated and envious and devotes her energies to putting glass door knobs throughout her colonial style bungalow! Although he imagines that another man might have been the making of Kitty, he fears that Rosamund would have destroyed Tom Outland. Indeed it seems as if Tom is better off dead than married to his daughter: '[He] would have had to "manage" a great deal of money, to be the instrument of a woman who would grow always more exacting. He had escaped all that' (261). Tom's sensitivity would, he feels, have been bruised by Rosamund and their marriage would have repeated the pattern of his own. But any woman would have disillusioned Tom: 'In personal relations he was apt to be exaggerated and quixotic. He idealized the people he loved and paid his devoir to the ideal rather than to the individual' (172). Though a more muscular version of Niel Herbert, he was clearly headed for a fall. In different ways, then, the Professor's relations with his daughters are difficult and it does not surprise that he cherishes the time when they were 'pretty little girls in fresh dresses' (101).

At times the Professor's deep-seated mistrust of women comes close to mysogyny. When he returns from his humiliating shopping spree with Rosamund, Lillian attempts to console him: 'Her heart ached for Godfrey' (155). He is 'warmed and comforted' by a good dinner and as they sit together in cosy domesticity she asks him what he is smiling about:

> 'I was thinking,' he answered absently, about Euripides; how, when he was an old man, he went and lived in a cave by the sea, and it was thought queer, at the time. It seems that houses had become insupportable to him. I wonder whether it was because he had observed women so closely all his life.' (156)

As the chapter ends here, one can only guess at the effect on Lillian of this bolt from the blue. She may, like the Wife of Bath before her, feel like hitting him on the head with the Collected Works. The Professor's Parthian shaft is characteristic of the first and final parts of the novel in which chapters do not draw to a conclusion, as is usual with Cather, but finish abruptly with either a cryptic statement or a question[11]: 'When a man had lovely children in his house, fragrant and happy, full of pretty fancies and generous impulses, why couldn't he keep them? Was there no way but Medea's, he wondered?' (126).

This is a very odd question indeed. Cather gives St Peter daughters not sons, so the disappointments of parenthood are placed in a specifically sexual context. Kathleen and Rosamund play Goneril and Regan to his King Lear: 'A man . . . could get from his daughter a peculiar kind of hurt – one of the cruellest that flesh is heir to' (155). But unless one resorts to the desperate and self-defeating measure of infanticide, they cannot remain children for ever. The invocation of Medea brings a complex range of associations into play. First, it is interesting that he should identify with the outraged and deserted wife, rather than allying himself with Jason and the claims of abused fatherhood. Moreover, Medea's 'way' is not designed to keep the children, only to deprive Jason of them. She is motivated by jealousy and revenge. That St Peter should see himself as Medea – one of the most terrifying, deranged and awe-inspiring characters in Greek mythology – suggests the intensity of the bitterness which lies behind the civilised exterior of the secondary social man.

The Medea who comes to mind is that of Euripides – whom the Professor cites as an anti-feminist authority while identifying with his most famous female character. In an article for *McClure's* Cather refers to the Euripidean conception of woman as 'an instrument, a thing driven and employed'; 'a disturber of equilibrium, . . . an emotional force that continually deflects reason, weary of her activities, yet kept within her orbit by her nature and the nature of men.[12] Cather offers this account of her sex without disparagement or comment of any kind but could she really have seen women in these terms? Characters such as Alexandra and Thea are certainly not 'instruments'; they have destinies of their own. Mrs Forrester, however, is cast in the Euripidean mould; indeed her tragedy is due to the confining orbit of sex. *The Professor's House* continues Cather's exploration of the perniciousness of sexual stereotype.

St Peter's reflections on Lillian mirror some of the ideas in the *McClure* essay:

> Her nature was intense and positive; it was like a chiselled surface, a die, a stamp upon which he could not be beaten out any longer. If her character were reduced to an heraldic device, it would be a hand (a beautiful hand) holding flaming arrows – the shafts of her violent loves and hates, her clear-cut ambitions. (274–275)

Lillian conforms to the Euripidean concept of woman as a disturber of equilibrium, an emotional force, but she is not a driven creature; rather it is the Professor who feels himself to be the instrument, beaten out and misshapen to accommodate her will. The passage employs an interesting reversal of imagery, with the conventionally female attribute of amorphous plasticity being assigned to St Peter while Lillian is hard, clear, defined.

The Professor and his wife are representative of their sex (and class); they are, in fact, strait-jacketed by the roles society assigns to them but in the course of the novel these categories are tested and questioned and, ultimately, refused. Even at the deepest psychological level Cather breaks down the conventional polarisation of sexual characteristics. St Peter exhibits the 'classic female forms' of illness: 'frigidity, depression, suicide attempts' and above all, passivity.[13] When he visits the doctor his symptoms, had he been a woman, would doubtless have been diagnosed as menopausal. In the first part of the novel the Professor fills out and is defined by his male role but in the final part, deprived of the trappings of masculinity, his condition is only and fully human.

The 'mistake' which haunts and eludes him is perhaps this, his inability to see beyond the orbit of a conventional masculinity. His recoil from the female sex is the result of his confused apprehension of the unsatisfactory relations between the sexes, translated into a scarcely conscious fear and resentment of women. This is illustrated by his attitude to the dressmaking 'forms' kept in his study. The first, which Augusta calls the 'bust', is a 'headless, armless female torso, covered in strong black cotton':

Though this figure looked so ample and billowy (as if you might lay your head upon its deep-breathing softness and rest safe for ever), if you touched it you suffered a severe shock, no matter how many times you had touched it before . . . . It was a dead, opaque, lumpy solidity, like chunks of putty, or tightly packed sawdust – very disappointing to the tactile sense, yet somehow always fooling you again. (18)

The bust, 'so richly developed in the part for which it was named' (17), is a maternal image, promising security and consolation. The language, particularly in the parenthesis ('as if you might lay your head . . . '), is charged with intense longing for the mother but she is a cruel delusion; alluring and repelling.

Although the second form is said to be 'more self-revelatory', it too deceives:

. . . a full-length female figure in a smart wire skirt with a trim metal waist line. It had no legs . . . no viscera behind its glistening ribs, and its bosom resembled a strong wire bird-cage. But St. Peter contended that it had a nervous system. When Augusta left it clad for the night in a new part dress . . . it often took on a sprightly, tricky air, as if it were going out for the evening to make a great show of being harum-scarum, giddy, *folle* . . . . At times the wire lady was most convincing in her pose of light behaviour, but she never fooled St. Peter, he had his blind spots, but he had never been taken in by one of her kind! (18–19)

At first sight it looks as if St Peter had never been taken in by a woman of light behaviour – that conventional snare of an innocent professor – but the pretence he sees through is merely the *pose* of giddiness and folly. Brittle, angular, nervous and, with her wire bird-cage bosom, almost sexless, she conforms to the image of the modern woman as neurotic, frigid tease; a direct descendant of Sue Brideshead in Hardy's *Jude the Obscure*.

Both the forms – the mother and the (fake) *femme fatale* – represent the stereotypes of femininity which inhibit St

Peter's understanding, but to him they only confirm his suspicion that women are not what they should be. More specifically, the bust is associated with Rosamund and her mother and the wire lady with Kathleen. Lillian's colouring is 'so soft that one did not realize, on first meeting her, how very definitely and decidedly her features were cut' (36). And Rosamund takes after her: 'usually' people are only aware of 'her rich complexion' and 'unresisting mouth' (59) but both Augusta, when she loses her savings, and the Cranes, discover how hard Rosamund can be. Kitty, who 'had the slender, undeveloped figure then very much in vogue' (37), mirrors the wire lady's pose of having a good time: 'There was something too plucky, too "I can-go-it-alone," about her quick step and jaunty little head' (64).

When Augusta comes to take the forms to the new house the Professor refuses to let them go, despite having complained of their being in his way in the past. He protests: '"I never complained, Augusta. Perhaps of certain disappointments they recalled, or of cruel biological necessities they imply – but of them individually, never!"' (21). Women, it seems, cannot help being women and it's really rather noble of him not to hold it against them! More seriously, his remarks serve as a gloss for the novel: the relations between the sexes are fraught with disappointments; to him this is inevitable, the result of 'biological necessity'. But the novel as a whole offers a critique of sexual relations and of the distortions that society imposes. When he declares to Augusta, '"You can't have my women. That's final"' (22), Cather highlights the problem. They are not *his* women any more than it is *his* house and the pain he suffers is the result of his possessive attitude. To the Professor, women, like the forms, are objects: he sees them only as they relate to him, never in and for themselves.

Behind the forms lies Anatole France's *The Wicker Work Woman* (1897). When Augusta apologises for their presence, St Peter retorts, '"If they were good enough for *Monsieur Bergeret*, they are certainly good enough for me"' (19). The Professor bears a marked resemblance to Bergeret, the protaganist of France's novel. Bergeret is a Classics professor at a provincial university where, like St Peter, he campaigns for high academic standards and is often in conflict with the administration. Bergeret has a study at home where he translates Virgil. It is an ugly, dark, cramped room ('la troisième chambre') which he shares with Madame Bergeret's dressmaker's dummy. The significance of this dummy is not at all ambiguous: 'There, bolt upright, over against the learned editions of Catullus and Petronius, stood, like a symbol of the wedded state, this wicker work woman' (94).

The story of Bergeret's domestic ills is narrated with unashamed masculine bias. Like St Peter's, his is a house of women but they have no redeeming features: 'His wife was a vulgar creature, who had by now lost all her good looks; his daughters, even, had no love for him'(11). So far as Bergeret is concerned his wife, Amelie, is 'just a paltry mind in a coarsened body' (11). She is stingy and slatternly; interested only in her social circle and contemptuous of her husband's work. Bergeret, like St Peter, has a favourite pupil, but M. Roux has none of Outland's innocence and charm. In fact, on returning home unexpectedly, he finds Roux and his wife in a 'compromising' position on the sofa. He is outraged and disgusted by her adultery and, although he had never loved her, he is bitter and disillusioned with womankind. Being of a reflective turn of mind, he ponders why he should be so upset and concludes that it is not in herself that Amelie is able to hurt him, but only as she is 'a symbol of Venus'. Seeing her in Roux's arms, she becomes an 'elementary type-form' and, he reasons, as 'an object of desire' she is bound to inspire 'either attraction or repulsion' (94).

Bergeret's meditations are close to the concerns of *The Professor's House*: both professors suffer domestic tragedy, both find women 'difficult'; both weary of the cycle of desire and disappointment which their sexual identity and the nature of women (as they conceive it) force upon them. But in comparison with Cather, France is crude and heavy-handed; he makes his professor indulge in seemingly interminable reflections on women and the symbolism he employs tends to be one dimensional. After catching Amelie and Roux red-handed, Bergeret repairs to his study and sees the wicker dummy. It reminds him of the 'hen-coops of the cottagers' (he is a hen-pecked husband) and the idol of woven cane in which 'the Phoenicians burnt their slaves' (he is a domestic martyr). 'Above all, the thing reminded him of Madame Bergeret, and although it was headless, he always expected to hear it burst out screaming, moaning, or scolding'(97–98). He crushes its 'wicker breast' and throws it 'creaking and mutilated' out of the window. There is simply no comparison to be made here with the subtlety and suggestiveness of the forms in *The Professor's House*.

*The Wicker Work Woman* is narrated exclusively from Bergeret's point of view. Moreover, France makes Amelie so unremittingly awful – cowardly, spiteful and stupid – loading the evidence against her and justifying (even relishing) Bergeret's loathing, it becomes almost amusing. Whereas Lillian and Godfrey suffer the mutual tragedy of falling out of love, the Bergerets had never loved each other from the beginning. In the end, Godfrey attempts to find an honourable solution but Bergeret scores a cynical triumph over his wife. He freezes her out of the house and gloats over her departure. It is not surprising that Cather thought there was more to say on this subject: *The Professor's House* is a reply to *The Wicker Work Woman*.

With Virginia Woolf's *To the Lighthouse* (1927), a third voice enters the colloquy. Although there is no actual allusion to Cather, Woolf knew her work well and there are obvious similarities between the two novels.[14] Both are about professors and their wives and children and in both the family house plays a prominent role. While Cather's novel may be seen as a corrective to France's, the figure of the professor remains central; it is still the historian, in a sense the artist, who claims her attention. She did not want to answer the character of Amelie with a portrait of a professor's long-suffering wife. In Woolf's novel, on the other hand, the professor, Ramsay, is a distant figure and attention is focused on Mrs Ramsay. The perspective is altered; aspects of Lillian's life which are only touched on obliquely in Cather's novel, form the staple of Woolf's. Lillian's unhappiness is voiced but it is not dwelt on. The strain of being a wife and mother, and specifically the wife of a man whose work forces him into isolation, is fully explored in *To the Lighthouse*. The difference in perspective is well illustrated in Ramsay's appeal to his wife:

> He wanted sympathy. He was a failure, he said . . . . It was sympathy he wanted, to be assured of his genius, first of all, and then to be taken within the circle of life, warmed and soothed, to have his senses restored to him, his barrenness made fertile, and all the rooms of the house made full of life . . . (39)

*The Professor's House* portrays the effect of the family on St Peter. *To the Lighthouse* renders the oppressive impact of Ramsay on the family. Both professors are dependent: St Peter had relished 'the warmth and fragrance in the air' stealing 'up to his study from the house below' and the knowledge that there were 'pretty little girls in fresh dresses', flowers, plants and a beautiful wife, waiting for him 'downstairs'(101). But though Cather questions this upstairs/downstairs relationship she would never have written, as Woolf does, of the 'fatal sterility of the male' or the 'delicious fecundity' of the female (38). To Cather, who consistently eschewed any overt connection with politics (sexual or otherwise), such terms would have been too specific.

In Woolf's novel the thrust of her argument is invariably apparent. Lily Briscoe, who chooses to be a painter rather than a wife and mother, must be continually assaulted by Charles Tansley's sneering, 'Women can't write, women can't paint' (81). Lily also provides a perspective on Mr Ramsay: 'he is petty, selfish, vain, egotistical; he is spoilt; he is a tyrant; he wears Mrs Ramsay to death' (27–28). And there is much in the novel to confirm her view. When, a few lines later, she tries to think of him as a professor not a husband, she admires his 'fiery unworldliness; he knows nothing about trifles'. But the reader knows that his lofty unconcern means that Mrs Ramsay must worry about the shabby state of the rooms that he wants 'furnished and full of life'; must fret over the fifty pounds to repair the greenhouse and feel 'the burden it laid on them' – herself and the children – that they had to 'hide small daily things' (41). Cather, however, is careful to show St Peter jumping into the chipped bath at night after work to give it another coat of enamel paint.

Woolf not only makes her professor a domestic tyrant but Mrs Ramsay a domestic martyr: 'They came to her, naturally, since she was a woman, all day long with this and that' (34). Naturally? Perhaps so, but then Mr Ramsay is hardly a sympathetic father. St Peter, on the other hand, spends one summer alone with his five-year-old daughter Kitty, working and caring for her, in a very happy arrangement. When his children grow up, he feels closest to Kitty. Without underlining the point, Cather suggests that the conventional relationship between father and child is neither natural nor inevitable, or even desirable.

Mrs Ramsay is continually expending sympathy: 'there was scarcely a shell of herself left for her to know herself by; all was so lavished and spent' (39). She is the living and never disappointing embodiment of 'the bust'. Even the objectionable Charles Tansley comes under her spell. But Woolf exposes the roots of his affection, showing how

Mrs Ramsay, in the cause of social harmony, flatters his vanity, appeases his wounded ego, 'insinuating, too, as she did the greatness of man's intellect'. The 'subjection of all wives' (15) is the basis of the Ramsay marriage: 'she did not like, even for a second, to feel finer than her husband'. She tries to hide his need, 'for then people said he depended on her' (40). Woolf emphasises the sexual politics in the family: the man egotistical, vain, demanding and the woman sympathetic, generous, drained.

One of the most important scenes in *To the Lighthouse*, occupying approximately twenty-five pages, is Mrs Ramsay's dinner party. Her Boeuf en Daube is a triumph. As she draws each participant out of their isolation and self-preoccupation into an harmonious group, the dinner becomes, as E.K. Brown points out, a kind of Communion.[15] The scene is set in a framework designed to emphasise its significance: 'But what have I done with my life? thought Mrs Ramsay, taking her place at the head of the dinner table' (78). During the dinner all the women play their part: Lily mollifies Charles Tansley, Minta is 'charming' to Mr Ramsay and Mrs Ramsay soothes Mr Bankes. Under her influence everyone is united but, as she leaves the room at the end of the evening, she looks over her shoulder at a scene 'which was vanishing even as she looked'(103).

Woolf attempts to capture the fugitive elements which make up a woman's life. Ordinary events are hallowed; cooking and caring for people is made significant. Mrs Ramsay's achievements are of necessity transient; the food is eaten, the children grow up and there are no books or paintings to show for it. But even after her death Mrs Ramsay is able to unite and console and, indeed, it is the memory of her which dominates the novel's final section. Towards the end, Lily realises that her great achievement was to make life itself 'a work of art': 'Mrs Ramsay saying "Life stand still here"; Mrs Ramsay making of the moment something permanent' (151).

Although the presentation of Mrs Ramsay sometimes suffers from an overkill of sympathy, Woolf's concern to celebrate the evanescent power and glory of a woman's life is wholly legitimate. Cather, too, valued domesticity and, in an interview entitled 'The Pioneer Mother', equated the woman's role with that of the artist. A character such as Ántonia has the same ability as Mrs Ramsay to create images which linger in the mind long after the moment has passed. Both writers gave something radically new to the novel but where Woolf performed a service for her sex consciously and, as her theoretical writings show, with polemical intent, Cather's female characters were born out of sheer affection.

However, in *The Professor's House* she had other purposes. She is less concerned with Lillian's special 'dinners' (109) for Scott and Louie than with the eight big volumes of her professor. St Peter has been engaged on an indisputably great piece of (creative) scholarly work but Woolf's professor has only 'reached Q' (35) on a scale of A to Z. Ramsay is tormented by self-doubt and is consequently vain and irritable. Woolf undermines the intellectual life, making it the product of male ego and sterility. All the academics display one or other, or both, of these qualities and Ramsay, Bankes and Tansley may be compared unfavourably with St Peter, Crane and Outland. While Cather gives her unqualified approval to the *Spanish Adventurers*, Woolf makes Ramsay's work faintly ridiculous by having Lily always think of it as 'a scrubbed kitchen table' (26). None the less it is his only justification: he is 'like a desolate sea-bird . . . marking the channel out there in the floods alone' (44–45). For this he commands respect but through his vanity, selfishness and childish temper tantrums, Woolf severely diminishes his stature. Someone who hurls plates across the room because there is an earwig in his soup had better get a little farther than 'Q'! Ironically, it is Cather who portrays the integrity of staying alone, in a room of one's own, and writing in it.

*To the Lighthouse* celebrates society, *The Professor's House* isolation; the fruitful solitariness of the artist. But is also about the price that has to be paid for this, by the spouse as much as anyone, and about ordinary human loneliness. In a speech given in 1937, Cather complained that 'the American novelist has been confined, or has confined himself, to two themes; how the young man got his girl, whether by matrimony or otherwise, and how he succeeded in business.'[16] In this novel she turns the American obsession with 'youth, love and success' on its head: it deals with growing old, falling out of love, the failure of success to bring fulfilment; the hollowness of the American dream. The only relationship that does not turn sour is Tom and Godfrey's and that is unsullied by sex or money.

The only moments of real happiness in the novel are achieved in isolation. St Peter says to Lillian that they should have been picturesquely shipwrecked together but when he considers 'the particular occasion he would have chosen for such a finale . . . his wife was not in it': 'Indeed, nobody was in it but himself, and a weather-dried little sea captain from the Hautes-Pyrénées, half a dozen spry sea-men, and a line of gleaming snow peaks, agonizingly high and sharp, along the southern coast of Spain'(95). The high-water mark of his life is not only when he is essentially alone but when he has around him the undisturbing presence of the male group. For Tom, too, his time of 'unalloyed' 'happiness' is spent on the Blue Mesa, alone: 'I can scarcely hope that life will give me another summer like that one. It was my high tide' (251). And nothing, one feels, that he might have experienced with Rosamund could have equalled it.

The next best thing to being alone for Tom and Godfrey is being with each other. When Lillian grows jealous, they meet 'in the alcove behind the Professor's lecture room'(173) and they spend evenings together whenever they can, drinking wine and reading Lucretius. The relationship survives because it is intellectual, Platonic. It has nothing to do with money or sex. St Peter hotly refuses to benefit from Outland's will: "'My friendship with Outland is the one thing that I will not have translated into the vulgar tongue'" (62). Although their friendship shares many of the qualities of a love affair – the two men spend idyllic summers together and after Tom's death Godfrey wraps himself in Tom's blanket, which had been just "'like his skin'" (130), and 'dreams' of his return (263) – there is nothing sexual in their relationship. That is its virtue: because they are friends rather than lovers, there is not marriage and children and ultimately, disillusionment.

It is perhaps sad that the only satisfactory relationship in the novel should be so completely divorced from the social and family context. There is no future for Tom and Godfrey, they could hardly have taken summer holidays together for ever, and partly because of this there is nothing for Cather to do with Tom except kill him off in the war. Alternatively, it may be only the tyranny of our culture which insists on perceiving human relations in terms of sex; our mania for boy meets girl. In this novel Cather began to break new ground, suggesting that there are other, fruitful and fulfilling kinds of human contact; an exploration which led her to the androgynous territory of *Death Comes for the Archbishop*.

'Tom Outland's Story', which is set in the American Southwest, is clearly a precursor to the novel of the missionary priests. Its function in *The Professor's House* is mainly one of contrast. The Professor's house and Marsellus's 'Outland' residence are implicitly contrasted with the houses of Cliff City, where man had carved out an existence in harmony with the environment. It deals with a time of cultural integrity, with America's Indian past, as opposed to its tense and fragmented present. Characteristically, Cather spoke of her intention in aesthetic terms; she wanted to achieve the same effect that she found in Dutch paintings of interiors in which there was a window with a view of ships and the sea: 'In my book I tried to make Professor St. Peter's house rather overcrowded and stuffy with . . . American proprieties, clothes, furs, petty ambitions and quivering jealousies – until one got rather stifled. Then I wanted to open the sqaure window and let in the fresh air that blew in off the Blue Mesa'.[17] 'Tom Outland's Story', purportedly written by Tom himself, is in clear, bright prose; full of translucent evocations of the landscape, the light, the climate.

This central section not only provides an escape from the cramped and stultifying conditions of urban life, but a further perspective on the theme of human relations. Out on the Mesa the erstwhile loner, Roddy Blake; Tom, who is an orphan; and old Henry, the English drunk, band together. Henry keeps house and they are described as a 'happy family' (198). In a novel so concerned with the family it is significant that the happiest one should be this all male household of misfits. The only woman there is a corpse whom they name 'Mother Eve':

> She was lying on a yucca mat, partly covered in rags, and she had dried into a mummy in that water-drinking air. We thought she had been murdered; there was a great wound in her side, the ribs stuck out through the dried flesh. Her mouth was open as if she were screaming, and her face, through all those years, had kept a look of terrible agony. (214)

Mother Eve acquires symbolic resonances in much the same way as Augusta's sewing forms. Missy Dehn Kubitschek is right, I think, to connect the wire lady, with 'no viscera behind its glistening ribs', to the mummy and the 'great wound in her side' where 'the ribs stuck out through the dried flesh.'[18] Further, given the source for the forms in France's *The Wicker Work Woman*, the suggestion that Mother Eve was probably murdered by her husband for committing adultery, comes as no surprise.

In *The Professor's House* there is no actual instance of marital infidelity, but there are several references to it and the forms and the mummy all quiver with suggestions of betrayal. Given her name, it is difficult not to associate Mother Eve with Henry's death from a rattlesnake bite. The serpent rears its ugly head and poor Henry writhes in horrible agony to his end. She is an agent of destruction: when they attempted to transport her, '"she went to the bottom of Black Canyon and carried Hook's best mule along with her"' (244).

But if Mother Eve is a symbol of female deceit and adultery she is also an image of terrible suffering and her mummified agony comments on the savage vengeance exacted on her. The human drama on the Mesa is a heightened, symbolic and violent counterpart to the civilised society of Hamilton. Mother Eve is another female object. In an effort to explain how much she means to him, Tom says he would sell '"any living woman"' (244) before he would sell her. But when she is sold she crashes to the bottom of the canyon, offering perhaps the last word on men's attempt to possess women.

Any estimation of Cather's treatment of human relations would inevitably be somewhat simplistic. She deals with a problematic question, subtly, in a searching manner that has complex implications. She was divided in her estimation of the novel: at the time she spoke of it as a nasty, grim little tale, the product of a middle-aged mood; later she thought it was underrated. It was, she said, born of really fierce feeling.[19] To me, *The Professor's House* is humane and disturbing, fascinating and transitional. It explores 'the dark forest' of the human 'heart' (95) but there is a glimpse of the 'blue and gold' landscape of *Death Comes for the Archbishop*. Cather penetrates deep into the labyrinth of desire and disappointment; she does not possess the answers but she finds a way to move on from darkness into daylight. Like her professor, she is outward bound.

# 7 The chemistry of colour:

*Death Comes for the Archbishop,*
*Shadows on the Rock*

> Your memories are like the colors in paints,
> but you must arrange them.
>> Cather to New York *World*, 19 April 1925.'

At the end of *The Professor's House* Godfrey St Peter is 'outward bound'. Having overcome his despair and longing for death, Cather intimates that he is destined for a new, though unspecified, kind of life. In *Death Comes for the Archbishop* it is as if he were reincarnated as Jean Marie Latour. Although one is an historian and the other a priest the two share many characteristics: they are both fastidious, cultured, tolerant, humane and lonely but, above all, they are artists. The Professor's History is not a dry, scholastic work but a product of intense personal feeling, in which events are arranged in an organic design, and the pinnacle of the Archbishop's achievement is the Cathedral at Sante Fé. But while St Peter is ultimately dissatisfied even with his books, Latour finds fulfilment.

Latour too has moods, like the Professor, of bleakness and despair, 'lying in his bed, unable to sleep, with the sense of failure clutching at his heart' (211). But whereas St Peter finds himself utterly alone, alienated from the rest of humanity and wearied by the futile

cycle of desire and disappointment, Latour can transcend
his 'personal loneliness':

> He sat down before his desk, deep in reflection. It was
> just this solitariness of love in which a priest's life could
> be like his Master's. It was not a solitude of atrophy, of
> negation, but of perpetual flowering. (256)

He is restored by the experience of divine love and
finds, in Wallace Stevens' terms, an 'imperishable bliss'.[2]
But for St Peter – a lapsed Catholic – there are only
fragile and flawed human relations.[3]

It is curious that Cather, not herself a Catholic, should
offer Catholicism as a consolation for, and even an alternative to 'worldly' life. Certainly she felt a tremendous
sympathy for the oldest church, both because it endowed
suffering with dignity and as the greatest sponsor of the
arts. *Death Comes for the Archbishop* is not a Catholic
book in any exclusive or propagandist sense, however,
and Cather is careful to make Latour's experience relevant
to non-Catholics as well.

For example, although it might at first seem that
the major difference between the Archbishop's and
the Professor's work is that of the secular and the
divine, Cather stresses that the Cathedral is the result
of Latour's human desire: it gratifies his '"taste"', even
his '"vanity"'. He is worried that Father Vaillant may
think him '"worldly"'(245). Not content with an Ohio
church, he employs a French architect to build in the style
of his beloved Midi Romanesque. The Cathedral is not just
a place of worship but a work of art in its own right. The
real discriminating factor is a question of form: between the
word and the artefact. It is significant that the Professor's
eight-volume History is of the Southwest, dealing with
those very 'legends and customs and superstitions' (277)
that the Archbishop laments never having written down.

Cather intends the reader to accept the Professor's book as a great work and yet she insists that its completion brings him no peace: it fails because of the limitations of language. This dissatisfaction with the word is again reflected in *Death Comes for the Archbishop*, in which architecture, sculpture and painting are consistently revered for their greater power of communication. Paradoxically, Cather's most beautiful writing was shaped when she had least faith in language and was trying to make prose as much like painting as possible.

In a letter to the editor of *The Commonweal* Cather explains her preoccupation with the Catholic missionaries in the Southwest. She was not attracted primarily by doctrine or morality but by the churches: 'the hand-carved beams and joists, the utterly unconventional frescoes, the countless fanciful figures of the saints'.

> I used to wish there were some written account of the old times when those churches were built; but I soon felt that no record of them could be as real as they are themselves. They are their own story, and it is foolish convention that we must have everything interpreted for us in written language. There are other ways of telling what one feels . . . [4]

But not for Cather whose only recourse was to written language.

Cather's preoccupation with 'other ways of telling' resulted in a highly original narrative method. At the time, this was held against her: reviewers complained it was hard to classify and could not properly be termed a novel. Cather countered by calling it a 'narrative'.[5] Admittedly it had to be called something, but this hardly seems more helpful. Narrative implies plot and a causal relationship between events, features which are conspicuously absent. Cather presents scenes and tells stories but one thing does not lead to another in the conventional novelistic sense.

History? Biography? Travelogue? It has been read as all three but no classification is entirely convincing.[6] Historical novels rarely dispense with chronology as completely as Cather does here. The Prologue opens with the date (1848), as does the first chapter (1851), but from then on exact references are rare until 1888, a few months before the Archbishop's death. Cather's treatment of time is like the Archbishop's at the end of his life: 'He observed . . . that there was no longer any perspective in his memories . . . He was soon to have done with calendared time, and it had already ceased to count for him' (290). He remembers his childhood as clearly as the recent past. In the same way, events in the book are all equally vivid and it matters very little whether the Archbishop visited Eusabio before or after Doña Isabella 'lied' about her age, or Padre Gallegos died. Indeed it is often hard to recall, for although the book is set in a specific period, temporal sequence is almost irrelevant.

Moreover, the main historical facts are referred to only briefly: there are passing mentions of the border disputes between America and Mexico, the Indian raids, the gold rush in Colorado, the Civil War and the dispossession of the Navaho but none, with the exception of the latter, impinges very forcibly. Cather's interest is in the local customs and legends; the kind of material which rarely finds its way into the history books. It is not, then, an historical novel in any conventional way. It tells the story of Bishop Latour and Father Vaillant and the stories told to them. For example, on his visit to the priest at Taos the Bishop hears 'the best account he had ever heard of the great Indian revolt of 1680' from Padre Martínez, who 'knew his country, a country which had no written histories' (152). Through this digressive mode, Cather is freed from chronology and can range at will from ancient Indian ritual, to the martyrdom of the Spanish missionaries, to the building of the Cathedral and back again and so convey the many layers of history which make up the country.

If there had been no 'written histories' at all, of course, Cather could not have written hers. Although she drew on her own experience in the Southwest, she was also greatly indebted to *The Life of the Right Reverend Joseph P. Machebeuf*, by William Joseph Howlett. Howlett's account of Father Machebeuf's and Archbishop Lamy's life in New Mexico provided Cather with the models for her protagonists, and as the Blooms have pointed out, with many of the main events. With the exception of Lamy's death occurring before Machebeuf's, Cather is faithful to her source. None the less the book is not biography, even in a veiled form. Despite flashes back to Latour's youth in France, it really only deals with ten years of his life. Books 1 to 8 are concerned with his experiences as a pioneer priest, then there is a gap of thirty years before Book 9 and his death. Although Latour is a sympathetic and convincing character – so too is Vaillant – Cather's interest is not simply in him but in his relation to the country. This is what had fascinated her about Archbishop Lamy: 'the daily life of such a man in a crude frontier society'.[7]

Latour provides a perspective on the surroundings: it is largely through him that the reader sees the landscape and the people in it. For much of the time he is on the move, travelling through the 'great diocese' on a mule and so affording Cather the opportunity for lengthy description. To Stouck, this aspect suggests that she was working within the tradition of American travel literature. To him, the richness of local detail, the fascination with different customs, the digressive and anecdotal form all belong to this genre. Yet the Bishop's feeling for the country is not that of the tourist and the depth of vision in the book can hardly be contained by the term travelogue. Further, it is not unified by mere locality: it has its own thematic coherence.

*Death Comes for the Archbishop* must, after all, be called a novel, using the definition which Cather, in some exasperation, offered at the end of her letter to *The Commonweal*:

But a novel, it seems to me, is merely a work of imagination in which a writer tries to present the experiences and emotions of a group of people by the light of his own.

For Cather this was true whatever the writer's 'method' and, from *O Pioneers!* onwards, she herself had always tried to find the form most appropriate to the subject. *Death Comes for the Archbishop* is yet another such experiment.

The novel's apparent simplicity is belied by the multiplicity of interpretations it has inspired. Critics have offered historical, religious and topographical readings: the Archbishop has been seen as both priest and pioneer.[8] All of these responses are valid and none is all inclusive. While accepting the impossibility of being comprehensive, it seems to me that the novel is fundamentally about art. Not only is this one of the major themes, but Latour is both an artist and a priest, and in construction and style the novel owes much to the art of painting.

The Prologue immediately establishes its importance. Three cardinals sit in Rome discussing the appointment of the first bishop to New Mexico, with the missionary, Father Ferrand. When Latour is nominated, Cardinal de Allande asks whether he has '"any intelligence in matters of art"' (11). As the significance of this escapes Ferrand, the Cardinal narrates how a missionary from New Spain once came to his great-grandfather's house to beg a picture for a mission church among the Indians. To his surprise and dismay the missionary chose a young Saint Francis by El Greco. When he tried to argue that a beautiful painting would mean nothing to the '"scalp-takers"', the missionary replied: '"You refuse me this picture because it is a good picture. *It is too good for God, but it is not too good for you*"' (12). And so saying, he carried it off to New Mexico where it was subsequently lost. This anecdote highlights the role of Catholicism in the novel, which is consistently presented as the guardian of culture, and is the first statement of Cather's belief in the universality of beauty and the supremacy of art.

Latour would certainly have recognised de Allande's lost El Greco had he seen it. His awareness of European culture is extensive. Indeed towards the end of the novel Vaillant wonders whether Latour's exceptional scholarship and 'delicate perceptions' (254) have not been wasted in such a rough country. But it is just these qualities which make him Cather's ideal pioneer, particularly because he is also sensitive to other traditions. On his missionary journeys, it is always the paintings and artefacts which first attract his attention: Jesus de Baca's wooden parrot at Isleta, 'the bird of wonder and desire to the pueblo Indians' (87); the church at Laguna, 'painted above and about the altar with gods of wind and rain and thunder, sun and moon, linked together in a geometrical design of crimson and blue and dark green' (90).

Cather's overriding interest in art and its history is particularly well evinced by the episode in which Latour wakes to hear the Angelus being rung on 'a bell with beautiful tone'. He relishes the sound and Cather evokes his appreciation in the most physical, sensual language: 'Full, clear, with something bland and suave, each note floated through the air like a globe of silver'(43). He detects an Eastern resonance and is delighted by its exotic history, tracing its descent from the Moors, from whom the Templars adapted the custom of the Angelus, to the Spaniards, who handed on their skill in silverwork to the Mexicans, who in turn taught the Navahos. For him, the bell is a sublime instance of the continuity of culture.

Cather invests Latour with her own expansive appreciation of art and the ability to make connections between cultures. Perhaps the best instance of this occurs in his meditation on the little wooden doll representing the Virgin Mary, which had been carved over two hundred years ago, and was still being richly dressed and decorated by the women:

> These poor Mexicans, he reflected, were not the first to pour out their love in this simple fashion. Raphael and Titian had made costumes for Her in their time, and the great masters had made music for Her, and the great architects had built cathedrals for Her. Long before Her years on earth, in the long twilight between the Fall and the Redemption, the pagan sculptors were always trying to achieve the image of a goddess who should yet be a woman. (257)

The doll was 'something to fondle and something to adore'. Cather said that all great art simplifies, and what Latour recognises, despite the diversity of form, is the continuity and universality of human aspirations; the yearning for beauty, for permanence and a sense of purpose. For Latour this has a spiritual significance; art and religion both satisfying an urgent human need. As the Professor says, they are the same thing, in the end. Wherever Latour finds the 'physical form of love'(219), whether directly under the auspices of the Church or not, that is art and is religion.

It is this emphasis on the physical form that makes Latour an artist. It also characterises his religious belief; an invisible God being too remote and intangible a concept to be grasped. Just as art attempts to arrest the stream of life, so religion tries to capture the spirit of divine love. Hence the dominance of the Virgin Mary: the most human manifestation of divine Pity. When Latour, for example, in one of his moments of bleakness and despair, finds the old bond-woman Sada crying outside the church, they are both restored by an experience of 'holy joy' as they kneel in the Lady Chapel:

> He was able to feel . . . the preciousness of the things of the altar to her who was without possessions; the tapers,

the image of the Virgin, the figures of the saints, the Cross that took away indignity from suffering and made pain and poverty a means of fellowship with Christ . . . . He seemed able to feel all it meant to her to know that there was a Kind Woman in Heaven . . . (217)

Latour and Sada are brought close to 'the Fountain of all Pity' by the *things* on the altar; the tapers, the figures, the Cross and above all by the image of the Virgin. In the same way, when Padre Herrera tells Latour about Our Lady of Guadalupe, it is the fact of her having physically appeared which is treasured. Afterwards, Latour and Vaillant discuss its significance, Vaillant maintaining that '"Doctrine is well enough for the wise, Jean; but the miracle is something we can hold in our hands and love."' Latour agrees but adds:

' . . . an apparition is human vision corrected by divine love . . . . The Miracles of the Church seem to me to rest not so much upon faces or voices or healing power coming suddenly near to us from afar off, but upon our perceptions being made finer, so that for a moment our eyes can see and our ears can hear what is there about us always.' (50)

What he says here might also be read as a description of the artist, the conditions needed for the creation of art, and its aims. In addition to this it may be noted that the miracle itself concerned painting. When the Virgin appeared to Brother Juan at Guadalupe nobody believed him, so to authenticate the miracle, she carefully arranged some roses in his mantle and when he returned to his Bishop and opened it there was instead 'a painting of the Blessed Virgin, in robes of blue and rose and gold' (49).

For Latour, art is not separate from the rest of life, something which is found only in museums and galleries,

but a part of the society which produced it. The paintings
and sculptures he finds in New Mexico, for example, are
invariably anonymous; not the expression of an individual
ego but of the aspirations of a people. Each culture finds
its own forms, often suggested by the environment. The
wooden statues of the saints which he finds in all the
Mexican houses reflect the conditions in the country.
The figure of St Jacques with a staff and wallet becomes
Santiago, 'wearing the costume of a Mexican *ranchero*'
and riding a horse (28). And in Taos he notes 'the
high colour that was in landscape and gardens, in the
flaming cactus and the gaudily decorated altars, – in the
agonized Christs and dolorous Virgins . . . ' (142).

The landscape is also, of course, God's creation. The
mesa plain is one of His unfinished works: it has an air
of 'incompleteness'; 'as if, with all the materials for world-
making assembled, the Creator had desisted, gone away and
left everything on the point of being brought together . . . '
(95). It may also contain signs from Heaven. When Latour,
who is 'sensitive to the shape of things' (18), is lost in the
desert he finds a juniper which 'could not present more
faithfully the form of the Cross' (19). He kneels before it and
prays for deliverance and shortly afterwards stumbles upon
the Mexican settlement of Agua Secreta. He accepts this as
a miracle, though not of a 'direct and spectacular kind'. It
is a miracle 'with nature' not 'against' it (29).

The emblematic tradition in Christianity allows Latour
to sympathise with the Indians' belief that their gods are
present in the landscape. Although, to Christians, the
house of God is the church, in a broader sense He is
present everywhere in creation. In the same way the
Indians' country 'was a part of their religion; the two
were inseparable' (294). *Death Comes for the Archbishop*
barely mentions the Indian crafts – those decorated pots
and water jars which figure so prominently in *The Song
of the Lark* and *The Professor's House* – exploring instead

the Indian relation to the land. What art and religion express for the European and the Mexican, the Indian finds in the cliffs and canyons and plains; venerating not man-made forms but the forms of nature.

When Latour visits Ácoma he wonders that men should think of living on the top of a rock, hundreds of feet in the air, without soil or water. But on the mesa, away from the warlike Navahos and Apaches, the Ácoma Indians had found 'the hope of all suffering and tormented creatures – safety' (97). The cliff dwelling provides them with the same assurance offered by religion: 'The rock . . . was the utmost expression of human need; even mere feeling yearned for it; it was the highest comparison of loyalty in love and friendship. Christ Himself had used that comparison for the disciple to whom He gave the keys of His Church' (97). The Indians may not compose masses or build cathedrals but they have their rock: 'The Ácomas, who must share the universal human yearning for something permanent, enduring, without shadow of change, – they had their idea in substance' (98). Art, religion and the country become the same thing.

As a Frenchman in New Mexico, Latour is the perfect vehicle for Cather's abiding preoccupation with the interaction of the Old World and the New. Where before she had focused on the European immigrant and the land, in *Death Comes for the Archbishop* she deals with the European missionary and the Indian. Characteristically, it is the cultural context which interests her. Latour is at various times attracted, repelled and mystified by Indian traditions and rites.[9] He respects 'their veneration for old customs' (135), their religion and their stubborn refusal to change. His horror at the expulsion of the Navahos from their home in the Canyon de Chelly, for example, has nothing to do with rights or boundaries: the injustice lies in the violation of ancient belief; 'They believed that their old gods dwelt in the fastness of that canyon; like their Shiprock, it was an inviolate place, the very heart and centre of their life'(293). Despite his admiration – for their strength, self-sufficiency, physical grace – they remain unknown; their culture completely alien to his. So much so that at Ácoma, he falls 'prey to homesickness for his own kind, his own epoch, for European man and his glorious history of desire and dreams' (103).

Another striking difference between the Indian and the European is their attitude to nature: 'just as it was the white man's way to assert himself in any landscape, to change it, . . . it was the Indian's way to pass through a country without disturbing anything'(233). Their architecture is an attempt to 'vanish into the landscape'; not to 'master' the environment but to 'accommodate' themselves to it (234). The European's 'glorious history of desire and dreams' has largely consisted of a desire to 'order' nature – whether directly in landscape gardening and architecture, or more abstractly by arranging and recreating it in words, notes and brush strokes. The Indian's 'ingenious' merger with the landscape is another kind of art.

*Autre pays, autre moeurs*, but Latour is a white man and desires to leave his mark. His one 'keen worldly ambition' is to build a cathedral in Santa Fé: 'As he cherished this wish and meditated upon it, he came to feel that such a building might be a continuation of himself and his purpose, a physical body full of his aspirations after he had passed from the scene' (175). The Cathedral belongs to the European tradition of art which has always reflected this projection of the ego and the yearning for immortality – in a more concrete form than religion can offer. Also, as so often in Cather, art is presented as a consolation for the disappointments in human relations: the Cathedral 'had taken Father Vaillant's place in his life after that remarkable man went away' (271).

The yellow stone out of which it is made (reminding Latour of Clermont) and its Midi Romanesque style might

seem out of keeping with the landscape – an imposition even
– but to Latour and his architect the building is a '"part"'
of the place.[10] This '"kinship"', however, does not
conform to the Indian concept of architecture. The setting
is almost excessively dramatic: 'the tawny church seemed
to start directly out of [the] rose-coloured hills', 'to leap
out of the mountains' like a scene painting in opera (272).
It is the highest achievement in Latour's life, representing
many years' work. When he returns to Sanata Fé to die, he
stops his buggy and sits 'for a long while, looking at [its]
open, golden face' (271) and wakes the next morning 'with
a grateful sense of nearness to his Cathedral' (273).

Latour, then, is an artist and the novel's form reflects
this. In the final section he undergoes a period of reflection,
surveying the 'great picture of his life' and contrasting 'the
shallow light of the present' with 'the old deep days' (290)
of his arrival in New Mexico, like a painter arranging
foreground and background.[11] And in the portrayal of his
life Cather attempts to approach the condition of painting,
in which everything is present at the same time. Writing is
of necessity linear but Cather dispenses with chronology so
that the reader's experience of the novel can come as close
as possible to that of a viewer casting an eye across a canvas.
The novel does not open with Latour's early years; on the
contrary, that is reserved for its closing pages, and it is
not only his history which is dismantled and distributed
across the pages but the country's: the final scenes depict
both Latour's youth in France and tell the story of the
Navahos, the earliest inhabitants of the Southwest. The
novel ranges through space and time, juxtaposing scenes
from the past and the present, the Old World and the New,
in a manner usually only possible in painting.

This particular use of contrast prompted Rebecca West
to compare Cather with Velasquez 'when he showed the
tapestry makers working in shadow and some of their
fellows working in shadow honeycombed with golden

motes, and others still further back working in the white
wine of full sunlight.'[12] It is significant that critics have
turned to painting in order to convey the novel's distinctive
quality. Cather herself claimed she was indebted to Puvis
de Chavannes:

> I had all my life wanted to do something in the style
> of legend, which is absolutely the reverse of dramatic
> treatment. Since I first saw the Puvis de Chavannes
> frescoes of the life of Saint Geneviève in my student
> days, I have wished that I could try something a little
> like that in prose; something without accent, with none
> of the artificial elements of composition.[13]

But Cather had written 'without accent' before: *My Ántonia*
in particular does not 'hold the note' or 'use an incident
for all there is in it'; qualities which she here ascribes
to the influence of Chavannes. The originality of *Death
Comes for the Archbishop* lies not merely in its surface
calm but its provenance in painting, which provided her
with a new prose technique. This is largely attributable
to Chavannes but not exclusively.[14]

Chavannes' work is characterised by a static and subdued
style. The colours tend to be muted, and the arrangement
of figures and setting is primarily decorative rather than
animated, creating an atmosphere of serene beauty. Cather's
affinity with him is understandable. (They were both,
incidentally, idiosyncratic and independent artists who were
misunderstood and neglected after their death.) Clinton
Keeler's essay on the subject pits the Impressionists and
James Joyce against Chavannes and Cather: the former
were taking 'new directions', the latter were harking back
to earlier forms.[15] But although Keeler stresses Chavannes'
debt to the Florentine Renaissance, art historians have
recently heralded him as an important precursor of the

modernists.[16] It is also surely arguable that Cather, while sensitive to tradition, struck out on her own, albeit in a less flamboyant fashion than Joyce.

Keeler points out certain similarities. Chavannes' mural is divided into four panels with a frieze; the central one portraying Geneviève's youth in Nanterre, with the outer panels showing scenes from her later life. This Keeler relates to the effect of tableaux in *Death Comes for the Archbishop* which is structured, he maintains, as a series of panels. He finds Chavannes' immobility and his use of 'flat tones' reflected in Cather's avoidance of 'internal conflict' and flat characterisation. While there is some truth in all this, the novel is more dynamic than Keeler allows. Latour and Vaillant may be representative types, as their names suggest, but they are not allegorical figures. Latour particularly is a living character with moments of doubt and despair and human longings but they are not, as Cather said, 'forced up'. Tension is not absent from the novel, it lurks beneath the surface: in the bloody rites of the Penitentes and the sinister mysteries of the Indian cults; New Mexico is in 'the middle of a dark continent' (21), inhabited by 'two savage races' (148).

The novel is perhaps self-evidently a series of scenes but its scope is wider than Chavannes'. To him, she owed the initial impetus for the novel just as Debussy, searching for a new operatic form, found in Chavannes the inspiration for *Pelléas and Melissande* – a work which floats without exaggerated climax or contrivance in an apparently seamless flow of melody. But, unlike Chavannes, Cather was portraying not just a central life but life in the Southwest and the connection between the two. She deals with the French, Spanish, American, Indian and Mexican and their surroundings. To encompass this demands a complex form: a patchwork, as A.S. Byatt suggests, rather than a panel.[17] Indeed, Cather's manner of handling such diverse material is almost cubist. In a letter to E.K. Brown she explained that her initial stumbling block to writing the novel was the heterogeneity of the material – the story of the Southwest involved too many individuals little related to each other.[18] Latour provides the peg on which to hang their stories, but this is only possible because his life is not narrated chronologically. Cather moves backwards and forwards in time, splicing her account with description, anecdote and legend. Out of the welter of possibilities in a country's history and landscape she selects only the most suggestive features, simplifying them, and rendering them in clear, bold strokes. And, as in a cubist painting, the elements are arranged intuitively rather than logically. Cubism was not concerned with a mimetic representation of reality and neither was Cather.

Only 'almost' cubist, however, for the novel has a definite beginning and end, a firm framework. Cather's interest in the movement is manifest in her recommendation of D.H. Lawrence's *Sea and Sardinia*. Although she did not otherwise care for his prose she praises this as an example of the language of cubism.[19] And how else could one describe her opening scene?

> As far as he could see, on every side, the landscape was heaped up into monotonous red sand-hills, not much larger than haycocks, and very much the shape of haycocks . . . . They were so exactly like each other that he seemed to be wandering in some geometrical nightmare; . . . Every conical hill was spotted with smaller cones of juniper, a uniform yellowish green, as the hills were a uniform red. The hills thrust out of the ground so thickly that they seemed to be push-ing each other, elbowing each other aside, tipping each other over. (17–18)

This is an abbreviated quotation but even so the use of repetition, to convey the sense of monotonous uniformity, is evident and the geometrical nightmare of thrusting cones must suggest a cubist landscape.

Cubism is often said to have begun with Cézanne's advice to Picasso to look at nature in terms of cubes, cones and cylinders.[20] The intention was to achieve a sense of solidity and depth, to avoid reducing nature to a flat pattern; a tendency which had crept into the work of Chavannes' followers. The physical, tactile quality of Cather's descriptions seems to owe more to Cézanne than Chavannes – in this evocation of a wild pumpkin, for example:

> Its long, sharp, arrow-shaped leaves, frosted over with prickly silver, are thrust upward and crowded together; the whole rigid, up-thrust matted clump looks less like a plant than a great colony of grey-green lizards, moving and suddenly arrested by fear. (88)

Moreover, Chavannes' 'pale, primeval shades', as Cather termed them, have nothing to do with the 'high colour' of *Death Comes for the Archbishop*.[21] Throughout the novel one is aware of the play of light – as on the road to Mora:

> There was not a glimmer of white light in the dark vapours working overhead – rather, they took on the cold green of the evergreens. Even the white mules, their coats wet and matted into tufts, had turned a slaty hue, and the faces of the two priests were purple and spotted in that singular light. (64)

The Southwest is a land of vivid tones: the steep 'carnelian' hills outside Santa Fé, with their 'pine splashed slopes' against a blue sky, create a vibrant background and the colours become positively violent during a storm: 'then the sky above the mountains grew black, and the carnelian rocks become an intense lavender, all their pine trees strokes of dark purple; the hills drew nearer, the whole background approached like a dark threat' (272). Cather's descriptions are full of movement and richly textured. She evokes the landscape by applying words like paint, arranging shapes and colours. On the wagon train to Santa Fé, for example:

> . . . Father Latour could distinguish . . . wave-like mountains, resembling billows beaten up from a flat sea by a heavy gale; and their green was of two colours – aspen and evergreen, not intermingled but lying in solid areas of light and dark. (22)

Interestingly, in an interview given at about this time, she spoke of her fictional aims and procedures largely in terms of painting:

> [It is] just as if I put here on the table a green vase and beside it a yellow orange. Now, these two things affect each other. Side by side, they produce a reaction which neither of them will produce alone . . . I want the reader to see the orange and the vase – . . . [22]

And it is this ability to make us see which makes *Death Comes for the Archbishop* so successful: more than any of her other novels it leaves the reader with vivid pictures, and though dialogue has its place, one remembers it less than in any of her other books. As with Jacinto and the Bishop whose 'usual form of intercourse' was 'silence' (92–93), the language does not call attention to itself; it is as if Cather were actually working with images and not words at all.

Cather claimed (in the same letter to E.K. Brown) that she had not consciously paid much attention to language but also admitted that one is not necessarily a good judge of one's own processes. When she came to this book she had behind her nearly forty years of writing – and of looking at art. The fact that she referred to so many painters in

connection with the novel confirms their influence: not
only Chavannes but Holbein – from whose 'Dance of Death'
she took the title – and Jehan George Vibert.

Vibert was a very popular French artist who flourished in
the late nineteenth century by producing large storytelling
canvases. He had a special fondness for clerical scenes and
Cather said in an interview that it was his 'The Missionary's
Story' that gave her the idea for the Prologue.

> It showed a gorgeously furnished room with cardinals
> in scarlet, sitting at ease with their wine, and speaking
> to them, . . . a pioneer priest.

His style was, she said, 'in the manner of the day'.
He was no revolutionary. It has been regarded as odd
that 'this painting, which has about as much appeal to
modern taste as button shoes, should have inspired Cather's
vivid prologue'.[23] Yet its old-fashioned air is precisely what
Cather needed. The prologue is in the same style. It evokes
the world of European civilisation to which Latour belongs:
safe, sumptuous, ordered, and its function is to provide
maximum contrast. From the view of St Peter's dome in
the afternoon light, Cather swings in the very next scene
to the 'geometrical nightmare' of a New Mexican desert.

It has been assumed that the style of *Death Comes for
the Archbishop* is all of a piece. Critics speak of its clarity
and simplicity and yet, despite its apparent homogeneity,
it contains several distinct styles. She employed various
literary techniques just as she drew on various schools of
painting. In the letter to the *Commonweal* she spoke of
using 'the old trite phraseology of the frontier' in order to
convey the pioneer priests' experience: 'Some of those time
worn phrases I used as the note from the piano by which
the violinist tunes his instrument'. But she did not sound
the same note over and over again. It is heard of course –
when Vaillant sets off on one of his missionary journeys:

'The wiry little priest whose life was to be a succession of mountain ranges, pathless deserts, yawning canyons and swollen rivers, who was to carry the Cross into territories yet unknown and unnamed, who would wear down mules and horses . . .' (41). But a little of that goes a long way.

There are strains of Romantic melancholy:

> The snow had stopped, the gauzy clouds that had ribbed the arch of heaven were now all sunk into one soft white fog bank over the Sangre de Cristo mountains. The full moon shone high in the blue vault, majestic, lonely, benign. (219)

There are also moments of rhapsodic lyricism, soaring at times to ecstatic heights – as in this description of waking in the air of a new country:

> Something soft and wild and free, something that whispered to the ear on the pillow, lightened the heart, softly, softly picked the lock, slid the bolts, and released the prisoned spirit of man into the wind, into the blue and gold, into the morning, into the morning! (276)

Cather's is a mixed mode: employing an omniscient narrator, who is none the less not wholly distant and detached; drawing on various styles yet making them her own. She herself, as she said to Van Vechten, is out of the picture;[24] but present everywhere in the single, unifying vision which is both large and concentrated. Like the Archbishop's 'mixed theology' (31), which accepts all forms of worship, she accepts all forms of humanity: miserly Father Gallegos; tyrannical and lascivious Padre Martínez, who sings the Mass with such conviction and beauty; gluttonous Fray Balthazar, sadly but justly toppled from his rock; vain Doña Isabella, one of Cather's lost ladies; the stately Eusabio and the 'hero' Kit Carson who

misguidedly persecuted the Navaho. In Cather's wonderful
gallery of portraits, none doth offend. In style and in
vision, *Death Comes for the Archbishop*, using the word
in its root sense, is a truly catholic novel.

After inhabiting a 'brilliant blue world of stinging air and
moving cloud' (232) in *Death Comes for the Archbishop*, it
is disappointing to be invited to take a 'seat in the close
air by the apothecary's fire'.[25] *Shadows on the Rock* (1931)
is a grey and somewhat lifeless book and it hardly consoles
the reader to know that the effect was intentional. Cather
thought it enough that she had realised her purpose and was
piqued that her friends all behaved, so she said, as if they
had ordered a highball and she had brought them chicken
broth.[26] But for a novel so concerned with the culinary art,
thin soup was an unfortunate choice of fare.

Many of Cather's cherished preoccupations reappear:
her love of French culture and the Catholic church;
her interest in tradition, exile and the frontier. Colonial
Quebec in the late seventeenth century allowed her once
more to take up the Virgilian themes, of *pietas* and the
transportation of household gods from the Old World to
the New, which she had explored in *My Ántonia* and
*Death Comes for the Archbishop*. But she offers few new
insights: the novel is less a further exploration of these
concerns than a reiteration of them. Indeed her treatment
of all the major themes is diminished in scope, power and
depth. Above all, it is narrower in sympathy.

*Shadows on the Rock* is set almost exclusively in Quebec,
confining itself to the small French community there, and
particularly to the Auclair family, with the occasional
flashback to their life on the Quai des Céléstins. The
scenes in Paris, however, do not function as a contrast to
life in Quebec; on the contrary, they emphasise continuity
and the lack of change. Whatever the continent, Cather's
concerns are the *salon* behind the shop and Madame

Auclair's ambition to 'make the new life as much as possible like the old' (23). And herein lie the novel's two main deficiencies: the reduction of culture to the merely domestic and an attendant insularity.

In a rather sad dilution of her Virgilian reverence for tradition Cather seems to confound household gods with household goods. The reader is told that Madame Auclair brought the latter with her – 'without [them] she could not imagine life at all' (23) – and throughout the novel one is kept informed of the state of the 'well-worn' carpet, the sofa, the dining-table, curtains and linen. (Cather even tells us how often the Auclairs change their sheets!) When, towards the end of the book, Auclair intends to return to France the furniture goes into a decline: 'Perhaps the sofa and the table and the curtains had overheard [him] say that he could not take them home with him' (225). When it transpires that the family is to remain, the furniture makes a speedy recovery: 'A little more colour . . . come[s] back into the carpet and the curtains' (249). Or so Cécile thinks, for it is to her that Madame Auclair entrusts the maintenance of '"our way"' (25). With true *pietas* Cécile cooks, cleans, observes the 'proprieties' and 'all the little shades of feeling which make the common fine' (25). But when a twelve-year-old girl wakes in the middle of the night because she is worried about the parsley, one suspects that the mysteries of the *ménage* are being taken a little too seriously.

This cult of domesticity would be less unacceptable if it were not so exclusive. It is not just that the origin of culture is apparently to be found in a salad dressing[27] – a vinaigrette, of course – but that no other country can make one like the French. This is why, as Madame Auclair explains, '"we are called the most civilized people in Europe and other nations envy us"' (25). The Auclair family regards Canada's indigenous population as '"poor savages"' (24) and Cather, too, has little to say about them. The broad sympathy with other customs and traditions, evinced in

*Death Comes for the Archbishop,* is entirely absent from *Shadows on the Rock* and the excitement of exploring an uncharted territory is replaced by dread of the unknown. The counterpart to New Mexico's desert is the Canadian forest but the Auclairs never venture near it: 'The forest was suffocation, annihilation; there European man was quickly swallowed up in silence, distance, mould, black mud, and the stinging swarms of insect life that bred in it' (7).

Only one journey is made in the course of the novel. The trapper, Pierre Charron, takes Cécile four miles down river to the settlement of Saint-Laurent to stay with his friend, Baptiste Harnois, but after two nights she begs to go home because she has to share a bed with the girls of the family who do not wash before retiring. Reflecting on her adventure from the safety of the *salon*, Cécile admits that the Harnois are 'kind' people, 'but that was not enough; one had to have kind things about one, too' (195). Things invariably take precedence over people in *Shadows on the Rock*, for out of pots and pans one makes not stew, or even chicken broth, 'but life itself' (195). It comes as no surprise that almost the only tears in the novels are the Virgilian, *lacrimae rerum*, dropped for the ships which bring supplies: 'It brought tears to the eyes to think how faithful they were' (205).

Despite superficial similarities, *Death Comes for the Archbishop* and *Shadows on the Rock* are fundamentally dissimilar. Unlike Latour, Auclair is an extremely reluctant pioneer. He is neither a priest nor an artist but an apothecary and a *petit bourgeois* who comes to Canada under the protection of Count Frontenac, his landlord in Paris, with whom he very much hopes to return. His interest in the New World is largely confined to its herbal life. He is without Latour's exceptional understanding of human nature, being merely decent, kindly and a trifle dull. Admittedly he is broad-minded enough to allow Cécile to play with the son of the 'bad' (50) woman of the town, but only because Jacques is a very devout little boy who is thoroughly ashamed of his mother. Cécile accepts unquestioningly her parents' standards and as she and Auclair provide the novel's point of view, all but the most conventional, Catholic and francophile reader is likely to grow restive before long.

That the culture she was describing was 'narrow' and the tone of her prose one of 'pious resignation', are facts to which Cather readily assented.[28] As she said elsewhere, to note a writer's limitations is but to define his genius,[29] but in this case hers are so severe that any definition could scarcely justify the name. The book is an aberration: the narrowness of vision is wholly uncharacteristic of her. After the novel's completion she seems to have had some doubts herself about the ethos which informs it, confessing to Governor Cross that 'the kind of feeling about life and fate' she found in Quebec was one she 'admired' but 'could not accept, wholly'. From the book itself, however, one would never guess that Cather had any reservations whatsoever about the Auclair 'way'. Moreover, it seems to me that there is something wistful in that 'wholly', as if she would have liked in her own life to have been able to conform to such a circumscribed view. It gave her, she said, 'a great deal of pleasure' to write about it.

The novel was written while Cather was at the peak of her career but at one of the lowest points in her personal life. In the summer of 1927 Cather had been evicted from her apartment on Bank Street by the construction of a subway. Houses were always important to her and she confessed to friends that the ordeal of moving was like having a funeral.[30] Perhaps the obsession with household goods owes something to the fact that hers were all in store. She could not face trying to find another home so she moved into the Grosvenor Hotel, New York, as a temporary measure – though this turned out to be her official address for the next five years. More importantly, in 1928, her father died of a heart attack and Cather was devastated. It has been suggested that the close relationship between

Auclair and his daughter was inspired by her affection for her own father[31] – though there seems little resemblance in character between Mr Cather, a humorous, gentle, and dashing Southern gentleman and Cécile's father.

The tragedy which really lies behind the novel is her mother's stroke and paralysis. Cather visited Quebec in 1928, the year her mother became ill. From 1929 until her death in 1931 – the year *Shadows on the Rock* came out – Mrs Cather lay immobile in a clinic in California. During this period Cather spent most of her time, either with her, or at the Hotel Frontenac in Quebec. The novel's stasis, its aura of chill petrification owe as much to her mother's paralysis as to the actual conditions of life in Quebec. Perhaps, indeed, paralysed by its climate and geography, cut off from the rest of the world for eight months of every year, Quebec provided Cather with the perfect analogue for her mother's illness.

Of the many stories and legends recounted (most of them Catholic in origin), the life of Jeanne le Ber stands figuratively and literally at the heart of the book. It tells of a beautiful, rich, kind and intelligent girl who insists on walling herself up in a little cell in order to devote herself to God. After twenty years, her childhood suitor, Charron, hides in the cold church where she prays each midnight. Her face had become '"a stone face"' and her voice, '"hoarse, hollow with the sound of despair in it"'. Charron is appalled; '"When she prayed in silence, such sighs broke from her. And once a groan, such as I have never heard; such despair – such resignation and despair!"' (180–181). Perhaps the quiet agony that Cather and her mother suffered, day after day for over two years, found expression in the legend of *la récluse de Ville-Marie*. But, when one considers the robust and sometimes even belligerent heroines of Cather's earlier years, it is chastening to find her endorsing Jeanne's renunciation; as if Cather, who had celebrated so much of life in her novels, really believed that in throwing away

the world Jeanne had made an 'incomparable gift' (135).
And even the more lively Cécile is reclusive; displaying an
almost neurotic need to be cocooned. She is utterly lost
without her home and familiar surroundings: 'All these
things seemed to her like layers and layers of shelter, with
this one flickering, shadowy room at the core' (156).

In *Death Comes for the Archbishop* the Ácoma Indians
cling to their rock for physical safety and to appease
'the universal human yearning for something permanent,
enduring, without shadow of change'. The rock of Quebec
has the same symbolic function: 'a crag where for some
reason human beings built themselves nests . . . and held
fast' (233). It is treasured by its inhabitants as a place
'"where nothing changes"' (275). At a time of anxiety
and upheaval Cather too seems to have found refuge there:
in the idea of the rock and in the actual writing of the book.
In the remarkable collection of letters which Cather wrote
to Dorothy Canfield, there is a very moving account of how
*Shadows on the Rock* helped her to endure her mother's
illness.[32] She speaks of the pain of watching a tall, strong
woman being fed with a spoon like a baby and of how utterly
hopeless her mother's condition is; she sometimes wonders
why they try to build up her strength. As for herself, she has
lost her bearings and can think of nothing but the general
futility of existence. She has nothing to say.

When Mrs Cather could no longer talk; Cather wondered
how her mother could bear to go on living. Through the
last three bitter years, she said, the novel had been her
rock of refuge: the only thing in her life that held together
and stayed the same. When her mother died, she wrote to
Canfield that she felt like a ghost. Sometime afterwards she
described more fully what Quebec meant to her: it always
gave her a sense of loyalty, of being faithful to something.
To recapture that feeling was all that she had tried to
achieve in the novel. Every little detail of the way the
people lived is from some old book or letter and the

search for all those little things helped her to hold her life together. She could form no critical estimation of the book: her only feeling about it was the kind of gratitude you feel for an old coat that has kept you warm.

The novel's emphasis on loyalty and changelessness, the impression it gives of being overburdened with the minutiae of daily life, can be traced back to Cather's own need. Despite its length, it seems to have been constructed on a minature scale. The vision of Quebec which emerges is of a rock covered in church spires, nunneries, convents and bishop's palaces; it is as if Cather had ordered the scenery into a contained child's world like Cécile arranging her little nativity scene for Christmas. Elizabeth Sergeant also testifies to the novel's therapeutic value:

> Willa had been, she told me, faced with a troubling inner division of her powers at this period . . . As the Pueblo male retires from the teeming village to the kiva or underground chamber, so she could find herself as an artist in her hidden imaginary retreat on the rock of Quebec, and emerge from it with the power to bring something vital to the life that clung to hers.[33]

If there is little vitality in the book – a fact which seems to be acknowledged by the title – this perhaps explains why.

By a curious anomaly, the 'inner division of her powers' of which Cather spoke, brought forth two works. Although *Obscure Destinies* first appeared in 1932, the stories themselves were written between 1928 and 1931. In these, Cather returns to childhood memories of her family and friends, to the world she had created in *My Ántonia,* only in a more directly autobiographical vein. Each of the stories ends in death, but they are as warm and golden as *Shadows on the Rock* is chill and grey.

# 8 Testimony:

*Obscure Destinies, Sapphira and the Slave Girl, The Old Beauty and Others*

> I have been running away from myself all my life . . .
>
> Willa Cather to Dorothy Canfield[1]

Spending time alone with her mother forced Cather into a new awareness of herself. She confessed to Dorothy Canfield that she seemed to have been a jumble of sensations and enthusiasms; not a real person at all. Until her mother fell ill, she had been so absorbed in her work, her friends, in listening to music, that she had given little thought to herself as a person; indeed, she had always deliberately avoided introspection and self-analysis. Although memory had played an important part in her life, she had never been concerned with herself in the past; that, she said, had always seemed to spoil things. But the last three years of her mother's life, she wrote to Canfield, held her close to herself, and it was like being held against things too sad to live with. But in the process of self-confrontation, it seems to me, Cather gained a new understanding of life; a kind of wisdom which makes her final books profoundly moving.

The last fifteen years of Cather's life is often described as a period of diminished creativity. She published *Obscure Destinies* in 1932, *Lucy Gayheart* appeared in 1935, *Sapphira and the Slave Girl* in 1940, and a collection of short stories, *The Old Beauty and Others*, was published posthumously in

1948. Critics have tended to envisage the line of her career as an arc which plunges downwards after *Death Comes for the Archbishop;* the general consensus is that she not only produced relatively little but that none of it is of her very best. This apparent falling off has largely been attributed to her alienation from contemporary society; it is held that she could not engage creatively with her own times and so was forced to beat a hasty retreat into the historical novel. Her reputation as a regional novelist has not helped either; it is argued that she had exhausted the prairie and the frontier and had nothing left to say. But in fact Cather's fictional territory is richly diverse; not only the Midwest but the Southwest, Pittsburgh, New York, Quebec and Virginia. And the quarrel with her treatment of the present is based on a misunderstanding of her novelistic strategy; she had never been inspired by recent events and circumstances but by the things which had 'teased the mind' for many years. Her material, almost from the beginning of her career, was filtered by time and shaped by memory.

It is largely because she has been seen as a conservative, regional novelist that her last works have been distorted and limited. She was never a consistently great writer; some of her early work, such as 'A Wagner Matinee' is extraordinarily fine, and some like *Alexander's Bridge* relatively undistinguished; *One of Ours* and *My Mortal Enemy*, written while at the peak of her power, do not equal her other works of the period; and at the end, although *The Old Beauty and Others* is a fairly weak collection, *Sapphira and the Slave Girl* is powerful if perplexing, and the stories in *Obscure Destinies* are extremely moving and finely balanced. This unevenness is attributable to her integrity. Each book is an attempt to capture an experience, a feeling or a particular quality and to portray it as vividly and authentically as possible. This entailed constant experimentation; each novel is a new departure and not every one is equally successful. Even at the end of

her life Cather never repeated herself or wrote to a formula.
She produced less because she was distracted by the death of
her brothers, Roscoe and Douglas; and old friends, among
them Isabelle McClung; and because she herself suffered
from various, minor but debilitating, illnesses.

Cather was quite capable of dealing with the present
but she did so in her own way. The chronicle of the
Depression, the portrayal of the horrors of the Second
World War, she left to others, as she considered that
immediate events were the concern of the journalist or the
polemicist. Although one could argue with Cather's attempt
to separate art from politics this need not inhibit our appreciation of her ideal – that art should be concerned with the
timeless and essential truths of the human condition. She
was not evading reality, or escaping from the complexities
of the moment, but searching her own experience for values
she could affirm. Moreover, although she did not address
the issues of her day directly she was, I believe, acutely
aware of them and these late works are informed by a
desire to speak up for the beliefs on which, it seemed
to her, civilisation depended. Simply, but not naively,
she tried to dramatise the necessity for certain fundamental
qualities: goodness, courage and human dignity.

In her last books Cather seems to complete a circle;
she returned to Nebraska and to her earliest experiences
in Virginia. But her treatment of memory is very different.
Although *My Ántonia* and *A Lost Lady*, for example, are
based loosely on people and circumstances she had known,
they are not autobiographical. Her later work, however,
is directly personal: she wrote to Violet Roseboro that
*Sapphira and the Slave Girl* is made up almost exclusively of
old family stories; the young Cather herself actually appears
in the epilogue when she uncharacteristically switches from
a third-person to a first-person narrator. Nancy and Till's
reunion, she said, was literally true, every word of it, and it
had been one of the greatest experiences of her childhood.[2]

It is almost as if she had a compulsion to testify to the things which had given meaning to her life. There is a new quality in the narrative voice; she had never spoken before as herself but here it is as if she were bearing witness. 'Two Friends', for example, is about the memory of two men, whom the narrator had known in early youth, whose friendship had suggested 'that there are certain unalterable realities, somewhere at the bottom of things'. They had seemed to the child large-minded and generous as they sat outside, talking, during the 'April nights, when the darkness itself tasted dusty', and the street was 'flooded by the rich indolence of a full moon, or a half-moon set in uncertain blue.' But the two men argued over politics and the friendship broke up, leaving the child with a sense of loss and regret. The story is a gentle warning against dogmatism and intolerance, spoken personally and with a sense of community with her readers: 'When that old scar is occasionally touched by chance, it rouses the old uneasiness; the feeling of something broken that could so easily have been mended . . . of a truth that was accidentally distorted – one of the truths we want to keep.'

Neither of the other stories in *Obscure Destinies* is told in the first person but they too are attempts to salvage the 'truths' that had been learned over a lifetime. In 'Neighbour Rosicky', Cather presents a picture of a farming family that is very similar to 'Cuzack's Boys' at the end of *My Ántonia*. However, the emphasis is not on the founding of a new civilisation but on the human qualities which make ordinary life fine. It centres on Rosicky's concern for his son and daughter-in-law who are newly wedded and struggling to survive. To encourage them, Rosicky and his wife tell stories about the hard times they had been through, of how one summer when the entire crop of corn had been burned and all the neighbours were discouraged and miserable, the Rosickys had taken a picnic and enjoyed it in the shade of the orchard. The couple had 'the same ideas about life' and agreed about 'what was most important and what was secondary'. They had never worried about putting money in the bank as long as they could maintain some 'sweetness' and '"style"' at home. When Rosicky becomes ill his daughter-in-law, Polly, grows closer to him and feels, she 'had never learned so much about life from anything as old Rosicky': it was as if he had 'a special gift for loving people, something that was like an ear for music or an eye for colour'. When he dies, his life seems in retrospect to have been 'complete and beautiful'; like a work of art.

In 'Old Mrs. Harris', the central character is also approaching death, with the 'kind of quiet, intensely quiet, dignity that comes from complete resignation to the chances of life.' Old, weary, and according to her neighbours, ill-used, Mrs. Harris is 'perfectly happy' when she is with her youngest grandchildren: 'they had in common all the realest and truest things'. The rest of the family are caught in that complex and troublesome time between adolescence and middle age; preoccupied and self-absorbed. The family is seen from various points of view. Mrs Rosen, who lives next door and befriends Grandma Harris, is exasperated by the parents' irresponsibility, the children's noise and mess and yet, though the family 'didn't seem to know there were such things as struggle or exactness or competition in the world', Mrs Rosen liked to go to the Templeton's more than other houses in the town: 'There was something easy, cordial, and carefree in the parlour . . . One felt a pleasantness in the human relationships.'

Victoria Templeton at first appears selfish and exacting; the neighbours disapprove of her because she goes out and leaves Grandma Harris at home to do the work. But as the story progresses it is revealed that her jealousy and irritableness are the result of her baffled awareness that she is disliked. Life had not turned out as she expected; brought up in the South where women were protected and admired, she cannot understand why, when she had tried to 'dress well' and 'keep young for her husband and children', she should find herself so unpopular. Her husband is not successful, there is never enough money and she discovers that she is pregnant again: 'She was sick of it all; sick of dragging this chain of life that never let her rest and periodically knotted and overpowered her'. But through Mr Rosen we also see her genuine fondness for her children and her charm; she has a 'good heart'.

Mr Templeton, gentle and unassertive, cannot cope with his ever-increasing family and decreasing means and periodically escapes to his farms in the country. Vickie is determined to do something with her life, frantically planning how she can make her way through college, and frustrated by her family's inability to support her. Full of their own affairs, nobody notices that Grandma Harris is dying:

> Thus Mrs. Harris slipped out of the Templeton's story; but Victoria and Vickie had still to go on . . . When they are old, they will come closer and closer to Grandma Harris. The will think a great deal about her, and remember things they never noticed; and their lot will be more or less like hers. They will regret that they heeded her so little; but they, too, will look into the eager, unseeing eyes of young people and feel themselves alone.

Again, it is as if Cather is speaking here, without bitterness or recrimination but with resigned wisdom.

Biographers have often remarked on the similarity of the Templetons to Cather's own family and suggested that, through the character of Vickie, she was trying to come to terms with the tensions that had existed in her relationship with her mother. Edith Lewis said that the story might well have been called 'Family Portraits'.[3] Given the nature of the material, it is not surprising that critics have tended to adopt a biographical approach to Cather's last books. The most convincing of these readings is offered by David Stouck, who suggests that at the end of her life, Cather reached a point where she no longer felt that art was of supreme importance, that she became more concerned with human relations and life and death.[4] *Lucy Gayheart*, he suggests, is a tragic account of the artist's life informed by an awareness of death. Clement Sebastian, who has dedicated everything to music, finds himself in middle age almost utterly alone. Cather concentrates not on Lucy's struggle to become an artist but on her failed love affair and her attempt to begin life again after Sebastian's death. The words which echo in the story are Mrs Ramsay's to Lucy: '"Nothing really matters but living. Get all you can out of it. I'm an old woman, and I know"' (165).

The 'selfishness' of the artist and the regret that Cather seems to have felt about her own inadequacies as a daughter, are the major themes which Stouck finds in these last works. He postulates that one of the most crucial factors in Cather's creativity was her relationship with her mother. In 'The Best Years', he says, Cather was again dealing with this theme but the conflict is gone. The story of the young Midwestern schoolteacher's weekend visit with her family is full of a joyous sense of homecoming: 'Lesley sat down on the porch floor, her feet on the ground, and sank into idleness and safety and perfect love.' Even the country is reassuring: 'the horizon was like a perfect circle, a great embrace'. And the mother has none of Victoria Templeton's imperiousness or selfishness: the children are united in their 'loyalty' to her and secure in the knowledge that 'Mother would take care of' everything. After Lesley's premature death, Mrs Ferguesson weeps for her daughter and, Stouck maintains, this 'affirms the deep feeling throughout the story that [Cather's] mother truly loved her.'

'The Best Years' was written in 1945 after Cather had made a visit to her beloved brother, Roscoe, and it may well have been an attempt to recapture the pleasure of growing up together. In *Sapphira and the Slave Girl*, too, Stouck sees Cather 'making her peace with life' and her family. Again the central characters, Sapphira and Henry Colbert, are said to be closely modelled on Cather's parents. But it seems strange that, between the forgiving portrait of Victoria Templeton and the adoring portrayal of Mrs Ferguesson, Cather should create such a forbidding mother figure as Sapphira. Certainly the novel is concerned with mothers and daughters – Till and Nancy, Rachel Blake and Sapphira – and with estrangement and reconciliation. However, it is the antagonism between Sapphira and her daughter which is dwelt on. Although Cather's novels have often been illuminated by biographical considerations, the danger is that the life can overshadow the work and sometimes even diminish it. The fact that critics have concentrated on Cather and her family has tended to detract from the scope of her last books – which do not show Cather's loss of faith in art but, on the contrary, her belief that art can, and must, sanction life.

If one leaves aside biographical considerations and concentrates on the novel itself, it emerges as a disturbing study of power with a particular relevance to her own time. *Sapphira and the Slave Girl* is set in antebellum Virginia; not in the milieu of Southern belles and chivalrous gentlemen but in the backwoods of mountain people and white trash. The only representative of polite Southern society is Sapphira; exiled from that world when she married 'beneath' her. Cather did not turn to Virginia because it represented 'a bastion of tradition in a changing world'[5] or because it afforded an opportunity for a nostalgic celebration of Southern manners. When a niece of hers moved South, Cather wrote in a letter that she was sorry to hear it; going South always sounded to her like going backwards.[6] And in 'Old Mrs. Harris' the South is described as 'primitive'.

In a letter to Violet Roseboro, Cather said that in a

narrative like *Sapphira and the Slave Girl* the trappings
(the customs and manners of the period) are easily come by.
But there is something else which eludes and eludes . . . the
Terrible, domesticated and a part of everyday life. That, she
said, is what she was thinking about.[7] It would be too easy
to make a simple identification of the Terrible with slavery
or even with Sapphira – though it has a lot to do with them
both. By 1940 there was no need for a crusading novel against
the injustice of slavery; what Cather probes here is rather
the implications for humanity that a slave-owning society
existed at all. The slow pace of the narrative, the period
detail and the digressions into 'local colour', all serve to
build up a picture of normality in which ordinary, decent
people go about their lives, accepting something monstrous.

Slavery is not just an issue in its own right, it provides
a means of exploring the psychology of domination and
paranoia. '"You're the master here"' (50), Henry Colbert
admits to his wife and, even though she is confined to a
chair, she rules her little world with an iron hand. She
controls the destinies of her slaves, deciding who may
marry, who she will sell and who keep. It is not that
she is unkind – Nancy, Till, Sampson, Fat Lizzie and
Tap are fond of her – but that she has power over them and
the desire to wield it. To maintain her dominion demands
constant vigilance; by making Sapphira an invalid, who
can never be sure what is happening outside of her room,
Cather increases the anxiety which despots inevitably feel.
Sapphira overhears Bluebell taunting Nancy with making
the miller's bed '"cumfa 'ble"' (61) for him, and sees
him talking earnestly with Nancy: 'Strange alarms and
suspicions began to race through her mind. How far
could she be deceived and mocked by her own servants
in her own house? . . . The Mistress sat still, scarcely
breathing, overcome by dread' (105–106).

Sapphira finally manages to call for help and Nancy's
and Till's prompt attention restores her: 'Her shattered,

treacherous house stood safe about her again. She was in her own room, wakened out of a dream of disaster' (106–107). Jealousy, here, is specifically a function of the will to possess. Although it is made very clear that the Colbert marriage is one of convenience rather than love, Sapphira is consumed with bitterness when she suspects something illicit in Henry's feeling for Nancy. As Henry will not allow her to sell Nancy she invites his younger brother, a notorious rake, to come to stay with them and insists that Nancy sleeps in the hallway where Mr Martin can get at her. She does everything she can to engineer Nancy's downfall. Cather equates slavery with rape – both being extreme forms of seeing people as objects – but perhaps surprisingly it is a woman, Sapphira, who shows the contempt for human life which both slavery and rape imply.

As Sapphira continues her malevolent and relentless pursual of Nancy (Martin is a mere pawn) the novel acquires a nightmare quality, filled with a child's helpless sense of fear. This atmosphere is heightened by images of troubled nights: Sapphira's 'dream of disaster', Nancy lying outside Sapphira's door kept awake by terror, the Miller up half the night poring over the Bible. Rachel and her father have to meet after dark to arrange Nancy's escape and Nancy's flight takes place in the middle of the night. When Rachel's children catch diphtheria she sits up watching over them through the small hours and her daughter, Mary, sleep-walks in her search for food. The novel reverberates with a sense of darkness, fear and subterfuge.

When Mary and Betty become ill the atmosphere changes. After Rachel helps Nancy to escape, Sapphira refuses to see her daughter but the death of her grandchild, Betty, brings about their reconciliation. Sapphira becomes suddenly compassionate, Rachel and Mary are invited to live at the mill and the nightmare dissolves. In the Epilogue, which takes place twenty-five years later, slavery has been abolished, Nancy and Till are reunited and harmony

prevails. But the Epilogue is like waking after a bad
dream when there is still a lingering sense of uneasiness
and inexplicable dread. The cosy picture of the women
sitting by the kitchen range, turning the bread and telling
stories about the past, is disturbed by earlier images and
memories of violence: the sound of Nancy being beaten by
a hairbrush, Till watching her mother burn to death, Jezebel
being flogged on board the slave ship – and the feeling that
the horror is not over. There is nothing sinister in the final
pages but, because Cather was so successful in conveying
the Terrible, it casts a shadow that the ending cannot quite
dispel, and she perhaps intended that it should not.

Although she began with the Epilogue – in 1937 –
the novel was not completed until 1940 and its dark
side seems to have been influenced by the threat of
war which hovered sinisterly over the final years of the
decade. In 1938 she wrote to Sinclair Lewis about her
concern for Americans' gullibility, their tendency to refuse
to believe evil exists, the excuses they make for Stalin and
Mussolini.[8] It is surely not coincidental that she chose to set
the novel in the period immediately before the Civil War, or
that Henry Colbert should be found reading the passage in
John Bunyan's *Holy War* 'relating to the state of the town of
Mansoul after Diabolus had entered her gates' (210).

The sense of malignancy is powerful but there are
forces in the novel working against it: not only Rachel
but Mrs Bywaters, Mr Whitford, David Fairhead and the
network of Quakers who help runaway slaves. Cather was
again, as she had been in *Obscure Destinies*, trying to speak
out for the values which, perhaps more than ever, she felt
needed to be affirmed. The difference between the two
works lies in the threat of evil that came with the onset
of the Second World War and which could not be ignored:
the miller does not want to see what is happening to Nancy
but 'he must face it' (227). There is a strong urge to believe
that the good will thrive: when young Casper Flight is

being tortured in the woods by a band of men, Rachel, old Mrs Ringer and her hunchback son, rush to defend him – a woman with 'two cripples' (127). Although the dangers and difficulties are not minimised, throughout the novel there are people who are prepared to make a stand for human dignity and freedom. Cather's friend, Dorothy Canfield, who reviewed the novel when it came out, declared that to 'readers of 1940' – 'helpless spectators of the horrifying spread of human slavery' – Cather had a particular message: 'the book bids us have faith.'[9] It was also a warning against complacency; an appeal to Americans to take note of what was happening in Europe.

The imputation of escapism, which many critics have made, is wholly unfounded; in *Sapphira and the Slave Girl* Cather was characteristically oblique, but she was not evasive. It can be read on several levels, and many of its complexities remain to be explored, but what always emerges is the reality of the Terrible and the validity of ordinary human struggle against it.

Understanding of Cather's last books has suffered from the assumption that she was an elegist of the past and nothing more: *Obscure Destinies* has been seen as a nostalgic glimpse of the prairies; *Sapphira and the Slave Girl* as an evocation of a 'vanished' beauty 'for which there was nothing to compensate' in her own time;[10] *The Old Beauty and Others* as an unpalatable compound of sentimentality and bitterness. Indeed, her reputation as a whole, from *My Ántonia* onwards, has been limited and marginalised by distorting categories: regionalism, conservatism, escapism. Despite this, and her temporary eclipse, people have gone on reading her novels and are doing so in ever-increasing numbers. If she has to be classified, let her be called a humanist. In a letter to Stephen Tennant, written towards the end of life, Cather replied to a query about the Great Tradition. The writers who last, she says, are the ones who are full-blooded and human enough to feed us; those that Fitzgerald called the 'helpers-to-live'. When she was ill, too ill even to eat, she read *The Canterbury Tales* and they made her want to get well and live.[11] Cather's work has the same life-enhancing quality and it will be read for as long as there are people to read at all.

# Notes

## Notes to Introduction

1. Interview by Eleanor Hinman, Lincoln *Sunday Star*, 6 Nov. 1921.

2. Most of the major surveys of modern American literature do not discuss Cather at all; when she does appear, it is invariably under the heading of 'Regionalism'. See W. Thorp, *American Writing in the Twentieth Century* (Harvard University Press, 1960), p. 55 and H. Straumann, *American Literature in the Twentieth Century* (Hutchinson's University Library, 1951), pp. 69–72.

3. In the correspondence between Randall Jarrell and Robert Lowell quoted by Ian Hamilton in *Robert Lowell: A Biography* (Faber and Faber, 1983) p. 180.

4. Comment by D. H. Lawrence on William Carlos Williams's *In The American Grain* (1925), quoted by A. S. Byatt in her introduction to the Virago edition of *Death Comes for the Archbishop*.

5. Virginia Woolf, 'American Fiction', *Virginia Woolf: Collected Essays* Vol. 2 (Hogarth Press, 1966), 113.

## Notes to Chapter 1

1. Willa Cather to Louise Pound. 13 Oct. 1897 (William R. Perkins Library, Duke University, Durham, North Carolina).

2. See E. K. Brown, *Willa Cather: A Critical Biography*, completed by Leon Edel (Knopf, 1953); James Woodress, *Willa Cather: Her Life and Art* (Pegasus, 1970); Phyllis C. Robinson, *Willa: The Life of Willa Cather* (Doubleday, 1983); Sharon O'Brien, *Willa Cather: The Emerging Voice*, 1873–1912 (Oxford University Press, 1987); James Woodress, *Willa Cather: A Literary Life* (University of Nebraska Press, 1987). Also, Edith Lewis, *Willa Cather Living: A Personal Record* (Knopf, 1953); Elizabeth Shepley Sergeant, *Willa Cather: A Memoir*, Bison ed. (University of Nebraska Press, 1963).

3. Willa Cather to Read Bain, 14 Jan. 1931 (Michigan Historical Collecitons, Bentley Historical Library, University of Michigan).

4. The mother/daughter relationship has received considerable attention from feminist critics. See particularly, Sharon O'Brien, 'Mothers, Daughters and the "Art Necessity": Willa Cather and the Creative Process', *American Novelists Revisited: Essays in Feminist Criticism*, ed. Fritz Fleischmann, (G. K. Hall, 1982), pp. 265–298.

5. See Mildred R. Bennett, *The World of Willa Cather*, Bison ed. (University of Nebraska Press, 1961).

6. *Writings from Willa Cather's Campus Years* (University of Nebraska Press, 1950), p. 15.

7. Willa Cather to Dorothy Canfield, [8 May 1922] (Bailey/Howe Library, University of Vermont).

8. Quoted by Woodress, *Willa Cather: Her Life and Art*, p. 55.

9. Quoted by Woodress, ibid, p. 56.

10. Willa Cather to Ned Abbott, 25 Oct. [1922] (Nebraska State Historical Society, Lincoln).

11. Willa Cather to Louise Pound, five letters, 6 Aug. 1892 to 13 Oct. 1897 (William R. Perkins Library, Duke University).

12. The information in this paragraph is taken from Cather's letters to Mariel Gere, four letters, 2 May 1896 to 25 April 1897 (Nebraska State Historical Society, Lincoln).

13. The chief exponent of this theory is John H. Randall III in *The Landscape and the Looking Glass: Willa Cather's Search for Value* (Houghton Mifflin, 1960).

14. Some feminist critics have also made damaging assumptions. See, for example, Deborah G. Lambert, 'The Defeat of a Hero: Autonomy and Sexuality in *My Ántonia*', *American Literature*, 53 (Jan. 1982), 676–690. Lambert states that Cather was a lesbian who could not acknowledge her homosexuality which she disguised in acceptable heterosexual forms. Both Lambert, and Carolyn Heilbrun in *Reinventing Womanhood* (Gollancz, 1979), assert that after her first novels Cather failed to portray strong, successful women and turned to male heroes. Lillian Faderman, too, suggests that Cather felt guilty about her lesbian emotions and that her 'suspiciously autobiographical' characters always appear as male 'whenever they show love interest in females', *Surpassing the Love of Men: Romantic Friendship and Love between Women from the Renaissance to the Present* (William Morrow & Co., 1981), pp. 201–202. Blanche H. Gelfant states that 'normal sex stands barred from [Cather's] fictional world', 'The Forgotten Reaping-Hook; Sex in *My Ántonia*', *Critical Essays on Willa Cather*, ed. John J. Murphy (G. K. Hall, 1984), p. 147.

15. Willa Cather to Edith Lewis, n.d. (Willa Cather Pioneer Memorial Museum and Educational Foundation, Red Cloud); three of McClung's letters to Cather escaped destruction and have been published by Marian Marsh Brown and Ruth Crone in *Only One Point of the Compass: Willa Cather in the Northeast* (Archer Editions, 1980).

16. Willa Cather to Elizabeth Sergeant, three letters about Julio, 21 May, 15 June, 14 Aug, [1912] (Pierpont Morgan Library, New York City).

17. Willa Cather to Dorothy Canfield, 17 April 1947 (Bailey/Howe Library, University of Vermont).

18. *Willa Cather: The Emerging Voice*, p. 4.

19. Lincoln *Courier*, 23 Nov. 1895, in *The Kingdom of Art: Willa Cather's FirstPrinciples and Critical Statements, 1893–1896*, ed. Bernice Slote (University of Nebraska Press, 1970), p. 409.

20. Willa Cather to Read Bain, 14 Jan. 1931 (Bentley Historical Library).

21. Willa Cather to Sarah Orne Jewett, four letters, 10 May [1908] to 17 Dec. [1908] (The Houghton Library, Harvard College, Cambridge).

22. 'How Willa Cather Found Herself', interview by Eva Mahoney, Omaha *World-Herald*, 27 Nov. 1921.

23. *Willa: The Life of Willa Cather*, p. 208.

24. Willa Cather to Zoë Akins, 20 May [1939] (Henry E. Huntington Library, San Marino, California).

25. 'Escapism', *Willa Cather on Writing* (Knopf, 1949), p. 27.

26. 'Escapism', ibid, p. 28; Elizabeth Sergeant, *Willa Cather: A Memoir*, p. 198.

27. 'Willa Cather Discusses Writing and Short Story Courses', [Nebraska State] *Journal*, 25 April 1925; 'On the Art of Fiction', *Willa Cather on Writing*, p. 103.

28. Cather's admiration is manifest in her letters to Thorton Wilder, two letters, 9 Oct. 1938 and 15 July 1940 (Beinecke Rare Book and Manuscript Library, Yale University); to Scott Fitzgerald, 18 April 1925 (PrincetonUniversity Library); to Sinclair Lewis, four letters, 14 April [1921] to 14 Jan 1938 (Beinecke Library). However, Elizabeth Sergeant relates how Cather disliked Lewis's *Main Street* when it appeared in 1920, *Willa Cather: A Memoir*, p. 166. For Cather's appreciation of Robert Frost, see Sergeant, pp. 213–214.

29. For Sinclair Lewis's comment see Mildred Bennett, *The World of Willa Cather*, p. 202; William Faulkner to Anita Loos, [1926] *Selected Letters of William Faulkner*, ed. Joseph Blotner (Random House, 1977); Scott Fitzgerald to Willa Cather, [late March/early April, 1925] *The Correspondence of F. Scott Fitzgerald*, eds. Matthew J. Bruccoli and M. M. Duggan (Random House, 1980); Wallace Stevens to Leonard C. van Geyzel, 9 Dec. 1940, *Letters of Wallace Stevens*, ed. Holly Stevens (Faber and Faber, 1967).

30. See Sergeant, *Willa Cather: A Memoir*, pp. 201 and 209.

31. 'The Novel Démeublé', *Not Under Forty* (Knopf, 1936), p. 55.

32. See 'Katherine Mansfield' and 'Joseph and His Brethren', *Not Under Forty*; Willa Cather to Stephen Tennant, [1939] (Wilsford Manor, Salisbury, Wiltshire).

33. Willa Cather to Dorothy Canfield [1933] (Bailey/Howe Library, University of Vermont).

34. Quoted by Edith Lewis, *Willa Cather Living*, p. 184.

35. Willa Cather to Zoë Akins, 28 Oct. [1937] (Henry E. Huntington Library, San Marino).

36. Sergeant, *Willa Cather: A Memoir*, pp. 251, 261.

37. Willa Cather to Harry Dwight, 20 July 1906 (Amherst College Library).

38. Sarah Orne Jewett to Willa Cather, 13 Dec. [1908], *Letters of Sarah Orne Jewett*, ed. Annie Fields (Houghton Mifflin, 1911).

39. Quoted by Bennett, *The World of Willa Cather*, p. 149; Yehudi Menuhin, *Unfinished Journey* (Macdonald & Jane's, 1977), p. 128.

40. 'Conversational Portraits', *Music for Chameleons* (Hamish Hamilton, 1981), p. 253–255.

## Notes to Chapter 2

1. Willa Cather to Will Owen Jones, 29 May 1919 (Clifton Waller Barrett Library, University of Virginia).

2. Willa Cather to Dorothy Canfield, [1933] (Bailey/Howe Library, University of Vermont). This chapter draws extensively on Cather's letters to Canfield. All references are to the Bailey/Howe collection.

3. [Nebraska State] *Journal*, 25 March 1894, in *The Kingdom of Art*, p. 187.

4. *Aspects of Wagner* (Alan Ross, 1968), p. 86.

5. *Wagner and Literature* (Manchester University Press, 1982), p. *xi*.

6. [Pittsburgh] *Leader*, 27 May 1899, in *The World and the Parish: Willa Cather's Articles and Reviews, 1893–1902*, ed. William M. Curtin (University of Nebraska Press, 1970), pp. 616–618.

7. [Lincoln, Nebraska] *Courier*, 10 June 1899, 'An Open letter to Nordica', *Courier*, 16 Dec, 1899 and *Courier*, 17 June 1899, in *The World and the Parish*, pp. 620–622, 642–646 and 625.

8. *Willa Cather on Writing* (Knopf), pp. 60–66.

9. *Courier*, 12 May 1900, in *The World and the Parish*, p. 658.

10. The phrase '"too much analysis kills"', is said by Madame Nordica and quoted by Cather, *Courier*, 7 June 1899.

11. 'My First Novels [There Were Two]', *Willa Cather on Writing*, pp. 91–92.

12. *The Troll Garden* (McClure, Phillips, 1905), reprinted in *Willa Cather's Collected Short Fiction, 1892–1912*, ed. Virginia Faulkner (University of Nebraska Press, 1970), pp. 149–261. This collection also contains 'Eric Hermannson's Soul' (1900), the first of Cather's stories to show Wagner's influence, pp. 359–379.

13. For his discussion of 'A Wagner Matinee', see *Music in Willa Cather's Fiction* (University of Nebraska Press, 1968), pp. 41–45. His study does not deal with Wagner's influence on Cather.

14. *Leader*, 6 March 1897, in *The World and the Parish*, pp. 402–404.

15. Quoted by William F. Blissett in 'George Moore and Literary Wagnerism', *George Moore's Mind and Art*, ed. Graham Owens (Oliver and Boyd, 1968), pp. 53–76.

16. *Leader*, 10 March, 1898, in *The World and the Parish*, p. 589.

17. George Moore, *Evelyn Innes* (T. Fisher Unwin, 1898), pp. 210–211. Subsequent page references are to this edition and will appear in the text.

18. Woodress, *Willa Cather: Her Life and Art*, p. 86; Randall, *The Landscape and the Looking Glass*, p. 45.

19. *Courier*, 12 May 1900, in *The World and the Parish*, p. 656.

20. Lionel Trilling, 'Willa Cather', *Willa Cather and her Critics*, ed. James Schroeter (Cornell University Press, 1967), p. 155.

21. Randall, *The Landscape and the Looking Glass*, pp. 46–47.

22. See Lewis, *Willa Cather Living*, pp. 92–93.

23. *Willa Cather: A Memoir*, p. 78.; for Fred Ottenburg's remark, see *The Song of the Lark* (Houghton Mifflin, 1915), p. 358.

24. For Landry's remarks, see *The Song of the Lark* (Houghton Mifflin, 1915), pp. 448–449.

25. For Thea's comment, see *The Song of the Lark* (Houghton Mifflin, 1915), p. 460.

26. *The Birth of Tragedy*, trans. W. A. Haussman, *The Complete Works of Friedrich Nietzsche*, ed. O. Levy (Foulis, 1909), Vol. 2, ch. 28.

27. 'The Novel Démeublé', *Not Under Forty*, p. 52.

28. Ernest Hemingway to Edmund Wilson, 25 Nov. 1923, *Selected Letters, 1917–1961*, ed. C. Baker (Granada, 1981).

29. Willa Cather to Elizabeth Moorhead [Vermorcken], [18 Sep. 1922] and [19 Sep. 1922] (Pierpont Morgan Library, New York City).

30. Willa Cather to H. L. Mencken, 6 Feb. 1922 (New York Public Library); Willa Cather to Carl Van Doren, n.d. (Princeton University Library, New Jersey).

31. Willa Cather to Mr Johns, 17 Nov. 1922 (Clifton Waller Barrett Library, University of Virginia); Willa Cather to Elizabeth Moorhead, [18 Sep. 1922] (Pierpont Morgan Library).

32. First published in *Woman's Home Companion*, 52 (Feb., March, 1925), reprinted in *Uncle Valentine and Other Stories: Willa Cather's Uncollected Short Fiction, 1915–1929*, ed. Bernice Slote (University of Nebraska Press, 1973), pp. 1–38.

33. *Music in Willa Cather's Fiction*, pp. 215–231.

34. *Willa Cather Living*, p. 173.

35. 'Friends of the Princeton University Library', 1933 (Princeton University Library, New Jersey).

**Notes to Chapter 3**

1. *Mid-American Chants* (Heubsch, 1923).

2. 'My First Novels [There Were Two]', (1931) *Willa Cather on Writing*, p. 94.

3. *The Works of Ralph Waldo Emerson* (Macmillan, 1912), Vol. 1, 91–92.

4. Hamlin Garland, *Crumbling Idols: Twelve Essays on Art Dealing Chiefly with Literature, Painting and the Drama*, (Stone and Kimball), pp. 13 and 10.

5. *Journal*, 26 Jan. 1896, *Journal*, 6 Jan. 1895 and *Journal*, 14 April 1895, in *The Kingdom of Art*, pp. 331, 219 and 223–224.

6. Willa Cather to H. L. Mencken, 6 Feb. 1922 (New York Public Library).

7. *Courier*, 30 Nov. 1895, in *The Kingdom of Art*, pp. 338–339.

8. 'My First Novels [There Were Two]', *Willa Cather on Writing*, pp. 93–94.

9. Willa Cather to Elizabeth Sergeant, 12 Sep. 1912 (Pierpont Morgan Library, New York City).

10. *Tar: A Midwest Childhood* (Boni and Liverwright, 1926), pp. 186–190. Subsequent page references are to this edition and will appear in the text.

11. Quoted by Marcus Cunliffe, *The Literature of the United States* (Penguin, 1954), p. 191.

12. *Literary History of the United States*, eds Howard Mumford Jones *et al.*, 4th ed. (Macmillan, 1974), p. 1216.

13. *The Literature of the United States*, p. 179.

14. Owen Wister, *The Virginian: A Horseman of the Plains* (Macmillan, 1949, p. 97).

15. Willa Cather to Mr Boynton, 6 Nov. 1914 (Clifton Waller Barrett Library, University of Virginia).

16. Willa Cather to Mr Gardiner, n.d. (Beinecke Library, Yale University).

17. Willa Cather to Zoë Akins, n.d. (Clifton Waller Barrett Library, University of Virginia).

18. *Courier*, 30 Nov. 1895, in *The Kingdom of Art*, pp. 338–339.

19. *Sketches from a Hunter's Album*, trans. Richard Freeborn (Penguin, 1967). Page references are to this edition and will appear in the text.

20. Willa Cather to H. L. Mencken, 6 Feb. 1922 (New York Public Library).

21. Willa Cather to Mr Miller, 24 Oct. 1924 (The Benjamin Hitz Collection, Newberry Library, Chicago).

22. *A Story Teller's Story* (B. W. Heubsch, 1924), p. 48.

23. 'Pioneers! O Pioneers!', *Leaves of Grass* (Airmont, 1965).

**Notes to Chapter 4**

1. Virgil, *Georgics*, trans. L. P. Wilkinson (Penguin, 1982).

2. 'The Originality of the Aeneid', *Studies in Latin Literature and Its Influence: Virgil*, ed. D. R. Dudley (Routledge and Kegan Paul, 1969), pp. 27–66.

3. Willa Cather to Mr Glick, 21 Jan. 1925 (Newberry Library, Chicago).

4. 'Arcadia on the Range', *Themes and Directions in American Literature*, eds Ray B. Browne and Donald Pizer (Pardue University Studies, 1969), pp. 108–129.

5. For a discussion of *My Ántonia* as a 'pastoral of innocence', see David Stouck, *Willa Cather's Imagination* (University of Nebraska Press, 1975), pp. 46–58.

6. Virgil, *Aeneid*, trans. C. Day Lewis (Oxford University Press, 1986), Bk. VI. lines 695–696. Subsequent references are to this edition and will be cited in the text.

7. 'The Classic Voice', *The Art of Willa Cather*, eds Bernice Slote and Virginia Faulkner (University of Nebraska Press, 1977), pp. 156–179.

8. Willa Cather to Mr Miller, 24 Oct. 1924 (Benjamin Hitz Collection, Newberry Library, Chicago).

9. Ántonia is so named in *The Literature of the American People*, ed. A. H. Quinn (Appleton Century Crofts, 1951), p. 908.

10. 'The Virginian and Ántonia Shimerda: Different Sides of the Western Coin', *Women and Western American Literature*, eds Helen Winter Stauffer and Susan J. Rosowski (Whitson, 1982), p. 176.

## Notes to Chapter 5

1. 'Willa Cather Discusses Writing and Short Story Courses', [Nebraska State] *Journal*, 25 April 1925.

2. See Dorothy Van Ghent, *Willa Cather*, (University of Minnesota Pamphlets on American Writers, no. 36, 1964), pp. 26–29; David Daiches, *Willa Cather: A Critical Introduction* (Cornell University Press, 1951), pp. 77–86; Edward A. and Lillian D. Bloom, *Willa Cather's Gift of Sympathy* (Southern Illinois University Press, 1962), pp. 67–74; John H. Randall, *The Landscape and the Looking Glass*, pp. 174–202; Leon Edel, 'Willa Cather: The Paradox of Success' and Granville Hicks, 'The Case Against Willa Cather', in *Willa Cather and her Critics*, ed. James Schroeter (Cornell University Press, 1967), pp. 261 and 143; Phillip L. Gerber, *Willa Cather*, Twayne's Series (Hall, 1975), pp. 109–112; E. K. Brown, *Willa Cather: A Critical Biography*, pp. 228–235.

3. 'Willa Cather's *A Lost Lady:* The Paradoxes of Change', *Novel* II (Fall 1977), 51–62; Kathleen L. Nichols, 'The Celibate Male in *A Lost Lady:* The Unreliable Centre of Consciousness', *Critical Essays on Willa Cather*, pp. 186–197.

4. 'Willa Cather Discusses Writing and Short Story Courses'.

5. *Willa Cather's Imagination*, p. 59.

6. Curiously, when Cather spoke of her debt to French prose in a letter to Albert Feuillerat in 1929, she did not mention Flaubert at all. (Sterling Memorial Library, Yale).

7. Gustave Flaubert to Louise Colet, quoted by E. Steegmuller, *Flaubert and Madame Bovary: A Double Portrait*, rev. ed. (Macmillan, 1968), p. 301; 'Willa Cather Discusses Writing and Short Story Courses'.

8. 'A Chance Meeting', *Not Under Forty*, pp. 1–46. Interestingly, Cather misremembered Flaubert's subtitle which is (the even colder) 'Histoire d'un Jeune Hommet'.

9. *Sentimental Education*, trans. Robert Baldick (Penguin, 1964).

10. Randall says that Cather demands that Mrs Forrester should 'commit suttee', *The Landscape and the Looking Glass*, p. 201.

11. Willa Cather to Zoë Akins, 19 April 1937 (Henry E. Huntington Library, San Marino).

12. 'Willa Cather Discusses Writing and Short Story Courses'.

13. 'The Novel Démeublé', *Not Under Forty*, pp. 47–56.

14. Willa Cather to Scott Fitzgerald, 28 April 1925 (Princeton University Library).

15. Eudora Welty, 'The House of Willa Cather', *The Art of Willa Cather*, p. 16.

### Notes to Chapter 6

1. Epigraph to Anatole France's, *The Wicker Work Woman*, trans. M. P. Willcocks (John Lane, The Bodley Head, 1924). Page references are to this edition and will appear in the text.

2. Virginia Woolf, *To the Lighthouse* (Grafton, 1977), p. 55. Subsequent page references are to this edition and will appear in the text.

3. In an interview entitled, 'The Pioneer Mother', Eleanor Hinman asked Cather for her views on careers for women in business and the arts: 'It cannot help but be good. It at least keeps the woman interested in something real. As for the choice between a woman's home and her career, is there any reason why she cannot have both? . . . If the woman's business is art . . . her family will be a help rather than a hindrance to her; and if she has a quarter of the vitality of her prototype on the farm she will be able to fulfil the claims of both.' Lincoln *Star*, 6 Nov. 1921.

4. Willa Cather, *My Mortal Enemy* (Virago, 1982), p. 105.

5. Quoted by Michèle Barrett, *Virginia Woolf: Women and Writing* (The Women's Press, 1979), pp. 26–27.

6. Lionel Trilling, 'Willa Cather', *Willa Cather and Her Critics*, p. 152.

7. Leon Edel, 'A Cave of One's Own', *Critical Essays on Willa Cather*, pp. 200–217 (Edel gives the date of McClung's marriage as 1917 but according to Sharon O'Brien's recent biography it was 1916, O'Brien, p. 239.)

8. 'Katherine Mansfield', *Not Under Forty*, pp. 153–154.

9. Quoted by Sergeant, *Willa Cather: A Memoir*, p. 215.

10. Willa Cather to Mr Bain, 14 Jan. 1931 (Bentley Historical Library, University of Michigan).

11. Fourteen out of twenty-two chapters end, either with a question, or the sound of a door slamming. Scott's comments are an example of the latter: '"Now what the hell is a virtual widow? Does he mean a virtuous widow, or the reverseous? Bang, bang!"' (p. 45).

12. Cather's reference to Euripides is made in the course of a discussion of Wagner's *Parsifal* in 'Three American Singers', *McClure's Magazine*, 42 (Dec. 1913), 33–48.

13. Elaine Showalter, *A Literature of their Own*, rev. ed. (Virago Press), p. 280.

14. Virginia Woolf mentions Cather in her essay, 'American Fiction', *Collected Essays*, Vol. 2, 112. See also Ellen Moers on Woolf's proposed article on Cather, *Literary Women*, 8th ed. (Women's Press, 1978), p. 239.

15. *Rhythm in the Novel* (University of Toronto Press, 1950), p. 66. Brown also makes a connection between *The Professor's House* and *To the Lighthouse*.

16. 'Friends of the Princeton University Library', 1933 (Princeton University Library).

17. 'On *The Professor's House*', *Willa Cather on Writing*, p. 31.

18. 'St. Peter and the World All Before Him', *Western American Literature*, 17 (May 1982), 15.

19. Willa Cather to Dorothy Canfield, 22 Oct. 1925 (Bailey/Howe Library, University of Vermont); Willa Cather to Elizabeth Moorhead, 5 May 1944 (Pierpont Morgan Library, New York City); Willa Cather to Irene Miner Weisz, 17 Feb. 1925 (Newberry Library, Chicago).

**Notes to Chapter 7**

1. Quoted by Bernice Slote in 'A Gathering of Nations', *The Art of Willa Cather*, p. 253.

2. 'Sunday Morning', *The Collected Poems of Wallace Stevens* (Faber, 1955).

3. *The Professor's House* is followed by the novella, *My Mortal Enemy*. Its protagonist, Myra Henshawe, is also a lapsed Catholic who falls out of love. Myra's return to faith shortly before her death marks, perhaps, a transition to *Death Comes for the Archbishop*.

4. Reprinted as 'On *Death Comes for the Archbishop*', *Willa Cather on Writing*, pp. 5–6.

5. 'On *Death Comes for the Archbishop*', *Willa Cather on Writing*, p.12. More recently, the narrative structure has received much favourable attention. See particularly Curtis Whittington Jr., 'The Stream and the Broken Pottery: The Form of Willa Cather's *Death Comes for the Archbishop*', *McNeese Review*, 16 (Spring 1965), 16–24.

6. For the novel as history/biography see E. A. and L. D. Bloom, 'On the Composition of a Novel', *Willa Cather's Gift of Sympathy*, pp. 197–236; as travelogue see David Stouck, 'Cather's *Archbishop* and Travel Writing', *Western American Literature*, 17 (Spring 1982) , 3–12.

7. 'On *Death Comes for the Archbishop*', *Willa Cather on Writing*, p. 7.

8. For a topographical reading see Judith Fryer, 'Cather's Felicitous Space', *Prairie Schooner*, 58 (1981), 185–198; for a discussion of Latour as a type of Aeneas see John J. Murphy, 'Willa Cather's Archbishop: A Western and Classical Perspective', *Critical Essays on Willa Cather*, pp. 258–265.

9. The most mysterious and sinister episode occurs in the chapter entitled 'Stone Lips'. Rebecca West compares Cather's treatment with D. H. Lawrence's probable approach: 'Mr. Lawrence . . . would have been through the hole after the snake', 'The Classic Artist', *Willa Cather and Her Critics*, p. 68.

10. Mary Austin in her autobiography, *Earth Horizon*, expressed horror at the building of a French cathedral in a Spanish town: 'It was a calamity to the local culture . . . It dropped the local mystery plays almost out of use, and many other far-derived Spanish customs.' Quoted by Sergeant, *Willa Cather: A Memoir*, p. 235.

11. For a discussion of the symbolic use of light see Clinton Keeler, 'Narrative Without Accent: Willa Cather and Puvis de Chavannes', *Critical Essays on Willa Cather*, pp. 251–257.

12. 'The Classic Artist', *Willa Cather and Her Critics*, p. 63.

13. 'On *Death Comes for the Archbishop*', *Willa Cather on Writing*, p. 9.

14. It is interesting to note that Flaubert's, *The Legend of St Julian Hospitator*, was inspired by a pictorial work; the stained-glass window in Rouen Cathedral which shows thirty scenes from the Saint's life.

15. Keeler, 'Narrative Without Accent: Willa Cather and Puvis de Chavannes', *Critical Essays on Willa Cather*, p. 252.

16. Richard J. Wattenmaker, *Puvis de Chavannes and the Modern Tradition*, (Art Gallery of Ontario, 1975).

17. See A. S. Byatt's introduction to the Virago edition.

18. Willa Cather to E. K. Brown, 9 April 1937 (Yale University Library).

19. Sergeant, *Willa Cather: A Memoir*, p. 200.

20. For this disussion of Cézanne and Picasso I am indebted to E. H. Gombrich, *The Story of Art* (Phaidon Press, 1953), pp. 432–435.

21. This phrase is to be found in an article called, 'A Philistine in the Gallery', signed 'Goliath' (*The Library*, 22 April 1900) which Bernice Slote identifies as being by Cather in her introduction to *The Kingdom of Art*, p. 78, n. 51.

22. Cather interview with Latrobe Carroll, 'Willa Sibert Cather', *Bookman* 53 (May 1921); quoted by Bernice Slote in 'Afterviews', *The Art of Willa Cather*, p. 253.

23. See James Woodress, 'The Genesis of the Prologue of *Death Comes for the Archbishop*', *American Literature*, 50 (1978–79), 473–478.

24. Willa Cather to Carl Van Vechten, n.d. (Boatwright Memorial Library, University of Richmond).

25. 'On *Shadows on the Rock*', *Willa Cather on Writing*, p. 16.

26. Willa Cather to Elizabeth Moorhead, 21 Aug. 1931 (Pierpont Morgan Library, New York City).

27. 'On *Shadows on the Rock*', *Willa Cather on Writing*, p. 16.

28. Ibid, pp. 15–17.

29. 'The Best Stories of Sarah Orne Jewett', *Willa Cather on Writing*, p. 54.

30. Willa Cather to Zoë Akins, [1927] (Clifton Waller Barrett Library, University of Virginia).

31. Woodress, *Willa Cather: Her Life and Art*, p. 237.

32. This, and the information in the subsequent paragraph, is from Willa Cather's letters to Dorothy Canfield (Bailey/Howe Library, University of Vermont).

33. Sergeant, *Willa Cather: A Memoir*, pp. 240–241.

**Notes to Chapter 8**

1. Willa Cather to Dorothy Canfield, n.d. (Bailey/Howe Library, University of Vermont).

2. Willa Cather to Violet Roseboro, 9 Nov. 1940 (Clifton Waller Barrett Library, University of Virginia).

3. *Willa Cather Living*, p. 6.

4. 'The Last Four Books', *Willa Cather's Imagination*, pp. 206–241.

5. Woodress, *Willa Cather: Her Life and Art*, p. 261.

6. Willa Cather to Irene Miner Weisz, 27 Feb. 1942 (Newberry Library, Chicago).

7. Willa Cather to Violet Roseboro, 9 Nov. 1940 (Clifton Waller Barrett Library, University of Virginia).

8. Willa Cather to Sinclair Lewis, 14 Jan. 1938 (Beinecke Library, Yale University). Susan J. Rosowski also relates the novel to the Second World War, *The Voyage Perilous: Willa Cather's Romanticism* (University of Nebraska Press, 1986), p. 243–244.

9. Dorothy Canfield's 1940 review is reprinted in *Critical Essays on Willa Cather*, pp. 284–286.

10. Brown, *Willa Cather: A Critical Biography*, p. 317.

11. Willa Cather to Stephen Tennant, [1944] (Wilsford Manor, Salisbury, Wiltshire).

# Bibliography

Page references in the text are to the
following editions:

*April Twilights* (University of Nebraska Press, 1968).
*Alexander's Bridge* (Houghton Mifflin Company, 1912).
*O Pioneers!* (Virago Press, 1983).
*The Song of the Lark* (Virago Press, 1982).
*My Ántonia* (Virago Press, 1980).
*Youth and the Bright Medusa* (Knopf, 1920).
*One of Ours* (Virago Press, 1987).
*A Lost Lady* (Virago Press, 1980).
*The Professor's House* (Virago Press, 1981).
*My Mortal Enemy* (Virago Press, 1982).
*Death Comes for the Archbishop* (Virago Press, 1981).
*Shadows on the Rock* (Virago Press, 1984).
*Obscure Destinies* (Knopf, 1932).
*Lucy Gayheart* (Virago Press, 1985).
*Not Under Forty* (Knopf, 1936).
*Sapphira and the Slave Girl* (Virago Press, 1986).
*The Old Beauty and Others* (Knopf, 1948).
*Willa Cather on Writing* (Knopf, 1949).
*The Kingdom of Art: Willa Cather's First Principles and Critical Statements, 1893–1896*, selected and edited with two essays and a commentary by Bernice Slote (University of Nebraska Press, 1966).
*The World and the Parish: Willa Cather's Articles and Reviews, 1893–1902*, selected and edited with a commentary by William M. Curtin, 2 Vols (University of Nebraska Press, 1970).
*Willa Cather's Collected Short Fiction, 1892–1912*, edited by Virginia Faulkner with an introduction by Mildred R. Bennett. Includes *The Troll Garden*, first published in 1905 by McClure, Phillips and Co. (University of Nebraska Press, 1970).

*Uncle Valentine and Other Stories: Willa Cather's Uncollected Short Fiction, 1915–1929,* edited with an introduction by Bernice Slote (University of Nebraska Press, 1973).

# Index